WITHDRAWN

DATE DUE			
Dec 15 78 B			
Nov 4 '80			

The Rise of the City Manager

The Rise of the City Manager

A Public Professional in Local Government

Richard J. Stillman II

UNIVERSITY OF NEW MEXICO PRESS

Albuquerque

For my parents

Where I belong and what I am living for, I first learned in the mirror of history.

Karl Jaspers
Origin and Goal of History (1953)

Men can know more than their ancestors did if they start with a knowledge of what their ancestors had already learned.

Walter Lippman
The Public Philosophy (1955)

Acknowledgments

I am deeply grateful to Dwight Waldo, the Albert Schweitzer Professor in the Humanities at the Maxwell School, Syracuse University. Dr. Waldo carefully read every chapter of this manuscript and gave substantial encouragement to the entire project. The late Professor Roscoe C. Martin, Professor Spencer D. Parratt, Dean Alan K. Campbell, and Dean Frank Marini of San Diego State University also offered helpful and stimulating ideas at various stages of the writing. Professors John C. Honey and Edwin A. Bock kindly sponsored my NASA University Fellowship at Maxwell which allowed me three years of uninterrupted study in the field of public administration. Samuel P. Huntington, the Frank G. Thomson Professor of Government at Harvard University, first fostered my general academic interest in the subject of public professionalism and Robert D. Balderston, colleague and friend, sharpened many of my ideas by his perceptive criticisms. Professors John C. Bollens, University of California, Los Angeles, Eugene Lee, University of California, Berkeley, and Ronald O. Loveridge, University of California, Riverside gave helpful comments on the final draft of the manuscript.

A number of city managers and former managers generously took time out of their busy schedules to aid my research, particularly Carleton Sharpe of Hartford, Connecticut; David Bauer, Wethersfield, Connecticut; Elisha Freedman, Montgomery County, Maryland; Bruce Clifford, Auburn, New York; Picot Floyd, Savannah, Georgia; and David Arnold, a staff member of the International City Management Association, Washington, D.C. Miss Betsey Knapp and the other staff members of the Maxwell School Library diligently tracked down several rather obscure documents.

Finally, a note of appreciation must go to the many scholars and practitioners who have labored in the difficult field of city management and local government. The citations in the text credit their enormous contribution to my understanding of the art and science of the field. Of course, what is written in these pages must ultimately remain the author's responsibility.

Chapter 4 of this study is based upon a paper the author delivered at the 1971 Conference of the Society for Public Administration in Denver, Colorado and has been published by the International City Management Association in a special monograph. The ICMA has kindly allowed me to use the same data in Chapter 4.

Contents

List of Tables

Introduction

For better or worse—or better *and* worse—much of our government is now in the hands of professionals.

Frederick C. Mosher,
*Democracy and the
Public Service* (1968)

The professions are being socialized and social and public professions are being professionalized.

T. H. Marshall,
Men, Work and Society (1962)

Profession . . . n. 1. a professing, or declaring; avowal. 2. an occupation requiring advanced academic training as medicine, law, etc. 3. all the persons in such an occupation.

*Webster's New World Dictionary of the
American Language* (1968)

Many social scientists would say that a study of the city manager belongs more to historians than to current research analysts. In part, they are correct. The council-manager plan was a product of the Progressive reform era and is now well over a half-century old. But the "manager phenomenon" is very much alive and well today. Statistics show that the plan has achieved its greatest period of growth in the post–World War II decades: the number of adoptions has quadrupled since 1945. Today approximately one out of four Americans lives in a manager community. There are nearly twenty-three hundred city managers in the United States, with managers in every state of the union except Hawaii and Indiana. Statistics also tell us that managers serve as chief administrators of 52 percent of American cities with populations of over twenty-five thousand, 50 percent of those over ten thousand, and 47 percent of municipalities over five thousand (although only 19 percent of American cities over five hundred thousand have managers and only 12 percent of those below five thousand are manager communities).

Moreover, a number of recent community power studies written by political scientists within the last decade tend to agree that city managers are not merely inconspicuous public administrators. Rather, these case studies conclude that managers *do* play influential roles in determining public policies within their respective communities. After a careful analysis of several council-manager cities in Florida, Gladys M. Kammerer, Charles D. Farris, John M. DeGrove, and Alfred Clubok found "no managers . . . who were not involved in the making, shaping or vetoing of policy proposals."[1] A similar study, conducted in North Carolina by B. James Kweder, pointed out that ". . . in many cities the manager clearly emerges as the person who has the greatest influence over what is happening at every stage of the policy-making process."[2] Aaron Wildavsky's *Leadership in a Small Town* (1964), which examined decision making in Oberlin, Ohio, revealed that the city manager was frequently a central figure in determining the outcome of important community policy issues.[3] Oliver P. Williams and Charles R. Adrian made similar observations: in two out of the four Michigan cities they studied, the city manager "was a key leadership figure and policy innovator."[4] Or, as David Greenstone wrote in his case study of San Diego, several of the community controversies that arose in that city during 1961 "were undoubtedly due to the political style of the City Manager, George Bean."[5]

Who is this central figure in American community life? How did his office originate? How did the city management profession develop? What are the characteristics of the modern city manager? This book attempts to answer these questions, which need to be answered simply because the city manager is an important public professional in American local government.

There are two other reasons, however, why the city manager merits careful scholarly attention today. One reason is that professional groups inside and outside government exercise widespread political influence in American society. As Frederick C. Mosher has pointed out: "For better or worse—or better *and* worse—much of our government is now in the hands of professionals."[6]

Certainly we read about the conflict between professionals and client groups nearly every day in the newspaper headlines—police versus minorities, public school teachers versus parents, welfare workers versus their clients, the military versus peace protesters, and nuclear scientists versus all of us. Professionalism seems to touch all walks of American life directly or indirectly, since today professional groups have considerable responsibility for determining the quality and standards of our public and private lives. Yet the striking fact is that we know very little about how professionals act, individually or in groups. We know, for example, a great deal from recent political science voting studies about how the American public votes, but comparatively little modern social science research has been devoted to analyzing how professionals determine public policies.

This book will attempt to examine one professional group, the city managers, who play significant policy-making roles in numerous American communities. How did their professional orientation develop? What are the basic components of their professionalism: their individual values, organizational structure, group ideology, external support, and social backgrounds? Have these components changed over the years? How does city management professionalism compare with that of other groups of public professionals?

Finally, and in the broadest sense, this analysis will be concerned with American history and political thought. It will attempt to place manager professionalism within the context of historic national values and culture. What were the ideas, events, and individuals that created and sustained manager professionalism? What forces have served to stimulate the growth and development of the council-manager plan and the city management profession? What are the present dilemmas and crises facing this group of local government public servants?

Chapter 1 traces the development of the office of the city manager as a unique product of the ideological and social milieu of the Progressive era. Chapters 2 and 3 examine the historic evolution of the managerial profession: its changing ideology, leadership, internal structure, and external support. Chapter 4 views the modern city manager by means of statistics, surveying his 1971 personal profiles, work habits, career patterns, and professional attitudes in comparison with those of the pre–World War II city manager. Chapter 5 studies managers on a cross-comparative basis, contrasting them with two other important groups of public professionals: career diplomats and public school superintendents. Finally, Chapter 6 concludes with an evaluation of city managers in the context of the pressing urban problems of modern American society.

Since the two phrases *council-manager plan* and *city management profession* will appear frequently, it may be worthwhile to distinguish between the two at the outset. The council-manager plan is a municipal reform doctrine developed by Richard Childs and sponsored by the National Municipal League since 1915. In brief, it establishes a method of community government with a directly elected city council and an appointed professional city manager. City councils under the manager plan are composed of five, seven, or nine members, elected either at large or by districts. They are responsible for setting the community public policies, passing ordinances, approving budgets, and appointing the chief executive officer, namely, the city manager, who serves at the council's pleasure. The mayor is normally elected from the council and, particularly in smaller communities, serves part time as a ceremonial leader. The full-time direction of the city administration is left to the city manager, who, in theory, carries out the policies of the city council and supervises the day-to-day operations of city administration.

The city management profession encompasses the professional association of managers. The manager plan serves as a model of local
government organization based upon a political doctrine; on the other
hand, the profession constitutes a recognized body of occupational
specialists whose full-time work involves municipal administration. Their
association was first formed in 1914 as the City Managers' Association, and
in 1924 it came to be called the International City Managers' Association.
In 1969 its title changed to the International City Management Association (ICMA). The ICMA publishes an official journal for its members,
first printed in 1919 as *The City Managers' Bulletin.* In 1923 it came to be
called the *City Manager Magazine,* and in 1927 it received its present title,
Public Management.

A final word to the reader: Before reading the text, it may be a good idea
to scan briefly the list of important dates provided in Appendix A. Because
of the numerous dates, events, and names that are frequently cited in the
text, the chronological table may help to clarify the sequence of topics that
are mentioned throughout the book.

1

The Origins and Growth of the Council-Manager Plan: *The Grass-roots Movement for Municipal Reform*

The position of city manager of course is the central feature of the council-manager plan and the ultimate theory of the scheme contemplates that he should be an expert in municipal administration, selected without reference to local politics. . . .

Richard S. Childs
National Municipal Review (1915)

Governmental problems have become intricate and even more insistent. They call for solution with the aid of science, not with the wisdom of a ward politician. The amazing mobility of the American people leaves no community a law unto itself; each and all are responsible for their own good government to the larger whole of which they are a part. What the whole world is witnessing is the emergence of government by experts, by men and women who are trained technicians highly specialized to perform some service by scientific methods.

Leonard D. White
The City Manager (1927)

The government of cities is an activity as old as the existence of cities themselves. The profession of city management, however, is a recent creation and a peculiarly American one. The idea of an appointed administrator for an American city can be traced as far back as President George Washington's suggestion to Secretary of the Navy Benjamin Stoddard in 1792: "It has always been my opinion . . . that the administration of the affairs of the Federal City ought to be under the immediate direction of a judicious skillful superintendent appointed and subject to the orders of the commissioner."[1] Congress failed to follow the president's advice, choosing instead to administer the capital by congressional committee. School boards, however, beginning with that of Louisville, Kentucky in 1837, hired trained educators to supervise their school systems, and by the mid-nineteenth century, forerunners of the modern professional public school superintendent appeared in a number of large American cities.

The development of the city management profession had to await the birth and growth of the council-manager plan in late nineteenth- and early twentieth-century America.[2] This chapter will examine the origins of the council-manager plan as the basis for the establishment of the modern profession of city management. The plan developed gradually; its growth can be divided into four separate phases: (1) the spread of the ideological and social roots of the council-manager plan; (2) the genesis of the manager plan; (3) the spread of the council-manager plan, (4) the evolution of spin-offs from the plan.

The Ideological and Social Roots of the Council-Manager Plan

The council-manager plan was a product of several ideas and forces that shaped late nineteenth- and early twentieth-century America. Among the factors that affected its development most significantly were: (1) the growth of urbanization; (2) the popularity of business and corporate ideals; (3) the Progressive reform movement; (4) the "scientific management" and public administration movements.

The Growth of Urbanization

Before the dawn of the twentieth century the famed historian Frederick Jackson Turner lamented that the closing of the American frontier marked the end of an important chapter in American history.[3] His views reflected the unease of many thoughtful Americans at the coming of the new age of urbanization, which dramatically changed the landscape of the nation between 1860 and 1910. During this half-century, towns and cities experienced miraculous growth. While the rural population doubled, the urban population grew to seven times its previous size. Urbanization swiftly converted villages into towns, towns into cities, and cities into metropolitan centers. Between 1880 and 1890, Chicago doubled its population and Detroit, Milwaukee, Columbus, and Cleveland each increased by 60 to 80 percent.

The rise of cities during this era was an involved phenomenon attributable to numerous economic and social forces: the decline of agriculture as the basic national occupation, the rise of modern manufacturing industry, the invention and subsequent demands for new consumer goods, an expansionary national trade policy, positive governmental and fiscal incentives for industrial growth, and a massive influx of overseas immigrants (by 1910, 13,345,000 foreign-born persons were living in the

United States, which amounted to almost one-seventh of the American population).

Whatever brought people to cities, urbanization placed new burdens on local governments throughout the country. Growing populations created new and greater requirements for public facilities. Lent D. Upson points out that between 1860 and 1910, 147 new activities were added to Detroit's municipal government, and in the next decade, 1910–20, another 81 functions were added, including development of zoning plans, inspection of food handlers, public health nursing, community centers, electric street lighting, motorized fire and police services, public airports, dental care for school children, mandatory grade school—and later high school—education.[4] The near-geometric increase in local public services gave rise to a need for specialized expertise to supply these new urban services; hence the creation of new occupational groups like the International Association of Chiefs of Police (1893), International Association of Fire Chiefs (1893), American Society of Municipal Engineers (1894), Municipal Finance Officers Association (1906), National Recreation Association (1906), National Association of Public School Business Officials (1910), National Organization for Public Health Nursing (1912). The demand for the specialized administrative skills of city managers, as we shall see later when we examine the case of Staunton, Virginia, was a similar response to the sudden requirements of urbanization.

The Popularity of Business and Corporate Ideals

Commercial activities have been one of the vital forces in shaping American society, and the businessman and the corporation have often been instrumental in determining public values. During the last years of McKinley's administration and the early years of Theodore Roosevelt's, when the great American corporate trusts were founded—among them U.S. Steel, Standard Oil, Consolidated Tobacco, and American Smelting and Refining—corporations were prominent, and the names of corporate "managers" like Rockefeller, Carnegie, Ford, and Harriman were household words. The novels of Horatio Alger, in which poor boy heroes acquired millions through hard work in business, were enormously popular. Historian David Potter aptly summarizes the influence of great businesses in that era:

> Government assured the new corporations, through judicial interpretations of the 14th Amendment, that they would enjoy the fullest legal security and even advantage; by the tariffs . . . it guaranteed the corporations control of the American market. In return they did what was expected of them: they converted potential wealth into

usable wealth, wastefully, selfishly, and ruthlessly in many cases, but quickly—and results were the primary thing demanded of them.[5]

The success of corporations in the private sector had a marked influence on American political and administrative thought. As Dwight Waldo observes, ". . . demonstrably the corporation both in its 'private' and public varieties, has influenced our administrative thought just as the institutions of the fief and the guild influenced medieval political thought."[6]

Probably no political or administrative philosophy reflects business and corporate ideals more clearly than the city management movement. Early writers on the subject frequently compared the citizens of a community to stockholders of a firm or the city council to the corporation's board of directors, and the city manager was often likened to the corporation manager. The very concept of a charter that centralized administrative authority under a single manager was closely related to the idea of a corporate charter that granted legal authority to a business firm. "Economy and efficiency," twin values of the business community, frequently found their way into the literature on city managers.[7] Here, for example, are the views of John N. Patterson on the advantages of the city manager concept for Dayton, Ohio in 1914:

> A city is a great business enterprise whose stockholders are the people. . . . Our municipal affairs would be placed upon a strict business basis and directed, not by partisans either Republican or Democratic, but by men who are skilled in business management and social science; who would treat our people's money as a trust fund, to be expended wisely and economically, without waste and for the benefit of all citizens.[8]

The writing of Richard Childs, often called "the father of the manager plan," is also heavily salted with business analogies:

> This [council-manager] plan corresponds to the general manager under the board of directors in a business corporation. It gives the stability of the combined judgment of many men on matters of policy, but leaves execution to a single-headed controlled executive establishment.[9]

The Progressive Reform Movement

Many of the effects of rapid urbanization and the rise of big business—particularly city bosses and conglomerate trusts—met with disfavor among a wide variety of persons, mostly professionals, who were known as Progressives. Richard Hofstadter observes that the Progressive reformers drew their greatest support from the more discontented native Americans and, on some issues, from the rural and small-town constituencies that surrounded the great cities. The Progressive philosophy, Hofstadter concludes, was:

> . . . founded upon the indigenous Yankee-Protestant political traditions and upon middle class life, assumed and demanded the constant disinterested activity of the citizen in public affairs, and argued that political life ought to be run, to a greater degree than it was, in accordance with general principles and abstract laws apart from and superior to personal needs. . . .[10]

In keeping with their "public-regarding" philosophy,[11] the Progressive reformers between 1900 and 1920 argued passionately for, and frequently won, many lasting legislative reforms, including antitrust legislation, short ballots, women's suffrage, anti–child labor laws, and home rule. One of the most significant municipal reforms developed and consistently supported by the Progressives was the council-manager plan. Leading Progressives such as Woodrow Wilson, Richard Childs, Charles Beard, and Clinton Woodruff became staunch supporters of the idea. The form and simplicity of the management concept ideally suited the Progressive philosophy: a competent manager would impartially and rationally administer public policy established by a nonpartisan council. What could be more "public regarding?" More disinterested? More abstract and universal? It was the very antithesis of the partisan big-city party boss that the reformers sought to destroy. The manager's apolitical qualities fitted the Progressive frame of mind, which favored impartiality and scorned personality politics.

Moreover, the manager concept was the perfect compromise between the two streams of Progressive thought, of which one saw the need for centralized planning and the other advocated decentralized grass-roots participation in public policy making.[12] Progressives achieved both of these seemingly contradictory ideas in the council-manager plan. On one hand, many Progressive writers, like Charles Beard and Herbert Croly, argued for a better planned, more rationally administered society that would resolve the pressing urban problems of the day. The manager plan would achieve this purpose by centralizing in the office of a single, trained "expert" the administrative functions of community government. Yet the commitment to grass-roots participation was not forgotten either. Boss rule was eliminated and power was decentralized by the election of councilmen at large, frequently on a nonpartisan ticket. Every citizen could be included in the policy-making process by way of the ballot box. Two apparently irreconcilable Progressive ideals, equality of participation and centralized administrative authority, were thus neatly balanced in the manager plan.

The Scientific Management and Public Administration Movements

The modern city management profession is also indebted to the currents and crosscurrents of academic thought in late nineteenth- and early twentieth-century America, particularly the scientific management and public administration movements.

The scientific management movement started with the research of Frederick Winslow Taylor to improve the efficiency of metal cutting and the production of manufactured units. By the time of his death in 1915 a new cult of "Taylorism" or the "scientific management movement" had attracted many disciples here and abroad (Taylorism became particularly popular in Russia during the 1920s). In its broadest form, the scientific management movement was a new philosophy that Dwight Waldo describes as a "mental revolution":

> One stands outside his material and contemplates it objectively. He discovers thus the true nature of what he regards, he discovers its laws. And he builds his system upon these laws. When it is done, it is not men or caprice nor will that rules: it is the System.[13]

Scientific management resembled earlier nineteenth-century British utilitarianism, pragmatic, scientific, and positivist in its orientation and outlook. It emphasized the achievement of specific results through the desired conditions of harmony, coordinations, economy, and efficiency. Good managers, proper planning based on the revealed principles, and adequate research into the "facts" of the situation were fundamental to the ideology of Taylorism.

Closely allied to the scientific management movement during the same period was a new consciousness in academic circles of a separate field of study, public administration. The classification of public administration as a separate field is normally traced to Woodrow Wilson's essay, "The Study of Administration" (1887). "Politics," Wilson wrote, "sets the task for administration," and administration involves the "detailed and systematic execution of public laws. Every particular application of general law is an act of administration."[14]

Wilson's essay today is considered the first to have pointed out the fundamental distinction between politics and administration, but, as Fred Riggs has written,

> Wilson was well aware of this interdependence. He never meant to imply that, in constitutional practice, a clear line could be drawn between political and administrative organization. . . . For Wilson not only were politics and administration closely intertwined, but administrative action was scarcely conceivable except as the implementation of general policies formulated by political means.[15]

Although Wilson envisioned a less hard-and-fast distinction between politics and administration, many administrative scholars, particularly between 1900 and 1935, saw a sharp division between the two spheres of policy determination and policy implementation. In 1900 this dichotomy was crystalized in a book by Columbia professor Frank J. Goodnow, *Politics and Administration:* ". . . In all governmental systems there are the ultimate functions of government, *viz.*, the expression of the will of the state and the execution of that will. . . . These functions are, respectively, politics and administration."[16]

How did the concepts of scientific management and public administration influence the development of the city manager movement? While it is hard to point to specific contributions, it is easy to note several connections among the kinds of thinking that led to these ideas. First, there was the similar faith in the application of scientific processes. The manager movement adopted a scientific, positivist spirit. City problems were considered solvable, and solutions could be discovered when an expert was put in charge. If enough thinking, planning, coordination, research, and efficiency were applied, practical answers, it was believed, could be found, even to difficult urban political dilemmas.

Second, as with Taylorism, the emphasis in city management was repeatedly on achieving results—practical, tangible, measurable ones. The purpose of the manager was conceived initially to be the achievement of definable objectives, frequently measured in terms of the values of "efficiency and economy." Third, the council-manager concept, like Taylorism, stressed the qualities of harmony, unity, and social solidarity. Especially in the policy-making process—deciding what should be done —the council was expected to set uniform policy guidelines for the manager to follow. In turn, the manager was supposed to have a free hand in policy implementation. Consensus was a dominant theme throughout the manager plan.

Finally, supported by much of the then-current academic literature in public administration, the council-manager plan drew sharp lines of demarcation between politics and administration. Politics and administration, it was argued, had separate spheres of influence in city government, and the two processes should not be confused. The council was responsible for policy making and the manager was primarily concerned with policy implementation, so the early theory ran.

The Genesis of the Manager Plan

The seeds for the growth of the city manager movement had been sown by a variety of forces existing in late nineteenth-century and early twentieth-century America: the rise of urbanization, the popularity of business and corporate ideals, the Progressive reform movement, the scientific management and public administration movements. The ground had been watered, so to speak, and now the process of germination was accelerated by several events: the creation of the National Municipal League and the commission plan, the Staunton experiment, and the work of Richard S. Childs.

The Creation of the National Municipal League and the Commission Plan

The National Municipal League originated as a confederation of local citizen reform clubs fighting big-city machine politics. The corruption of the spoils system was their major target; their goal, as once voiced by a leading Progressive, Woodrow Wilson, was "to set up a government where the average man, the plain man, the common man, the ignorant man, the unaccomplished man, the poor man had a voice equal to the voice of anybody else in the settling of community affairs. . . ."[17]

Encouraged by the exposés of journalist muckrakers of the late nineteenth century on the corruption of the big-city machines, reformers joined ranks in citizen associations in order to elect honest and competent officials to public office. The Committee of Seventy in New York City in the 1870s was the earliest "good government association" and it successfully overthrew the corrupt Tweed Ring. A similar group was later established in Philadelphia, and these two organizations met for the first time in 1894. This Good Government Conference laid the basis for the founding in 1895 of the National Municipal League, which served to bring together into one national organization the forty-six local government reform groups then in existence throughout the country.[18]

These reformers had as their original goals ending boss rule and electing honest men to city hall. Early in their activities, however, they recognized the need for changes in the basic structure of city government in order to make cities less prone to corrupt party influence. In 1898 the league approved the first model city charter as part of its general "Municipal Program of the National Municipal League." The model city charter offered what reformers saw as the ideal form of local government, essentially a strong-mayor type that concentrated executive powers in the elected executive. The model charter gave the mayor the authority to appoint his principal subordinates and to exercise control over the various city departments, boards, and committees. Legislative powers were concentrated in a unicameral legislature. Thus, through the concentration of authority in the elected officials, the reformers sought to destroy the backroom power of the city boss and make direct access to city hall available to more people.

Although the reformers sponsored the strong-mayor form, another kind of municipal government soon caught the eye of many of the league's supporters, and many of the league's local chapters began to give it considerable support. In 1900, a hurricane devastated much of Galveston, Texas and prompted a number of prominent Galveston businessmen to sponsor a new form of municipal government modeled along the lines of a business corporation. The commission plan adopted by Galveston in 1901 unified all powers of municipal government in a single, small body of five commissioners, directly elected by the citizenry. The commissioners were responsible individually for supervising the city departments and collectively for setting legislative policy for the community. Commission government completely abandoned the idea of separation of powers: the commissioners served both as legislators, passing on city ordinances and other legislation, and as chief executives, individually responsible for the line operations of municipal departments. Commission government was therefore the extreme form of centralizing administrative authority in a small group of political executives.

The commission plan quickly achieved considerable popularity and reform support. Ten years after it was first adopted in Galveston, commission government had spread to 160 cities around the United States.[19]

The Staunton Experiment

In 1906 Staunton, Virginia, a town of 11,336 people at the head of the Shenandoah Valley (and the birthplace of Woodrow Wilson), became a first-class city under Virginia state law. Having passed the 10,000 population mark according to a recent census, the community was forced to reorganize its government from a unicameral to a bicameral legislative body. The new bicameral city council was increased from twelve to twenty-two members, and the municipal government came under the direction of thirty legislative committees.

At that time Staunton had no full-time municipal employees, and the enlargement of its government brought what work was being done almost to a standstill; as one commentator observed, no one could agree on what should be done or how the work should be administered, and this left "the various city departments drifting without leadership."[20] A modern observer might term it the classic case of "excessive participatory democracy."

Moreover, an enormous backlog of public works projects awaited action. Eyewitness Henry Oyen graphically described the condition of the city streets:

> Each of the streets had a single streetcar track laid on ties only, at one side. The rest were plain mud. In wet weather wagons went hub

deep in the mire and it was a feat to make the crossing on foot. As for
the side streets, picture a red clay country road with a gully washed
out in the middle. . . .[21]

With the streets in a mess and the city government in a state of
inactivity, on August 7, 1906 a committee of the city council recommended as a practical solution for Staunton's problems that a position of
"municipal director" be created and that "all administrative work of the
city be placed in the hands of some competent salaried official. . . ."[22] But
this report was sidetracked while another legislative committee examined
the commission plan as an alternative solution. After a year of careful
study, the legislative committee concluded that adopting the commission
plan was not feasible. For one thing, it would add five new commissioners
to the existing unwieldy bicameral legislature, thus compounding the
present administrative chaos. Since the commission plan was found to be
unconstitutional under Virginia law, the summary report concluded that a
"general manager" of Staunton should be appointed, and on January 16,
1908 the two bodies of the city council passed an ordinance establishing an
office of "general manager," who would "have entire charge and control of
all executive work of the city in its various departments."[23]

It is clear from the tenor of the arguments presented that many of the
supporters of the "general manager" plan wanted the city to run in a more
businesslike manner. Its major sponsor, Councilman Hugh C. Braxton,
contended, ". . . Regarding Staunton simply as a business corporation . . .
it is evident that the same principles should be applied as would be applied
in the case of any ordinary business concern."[24] Editorial comment in the
Staunton Daily Leader also backed the same "self-evident" business
principles: ". . . A municipal director is a man who has charge of and runs
the city on business-like principles. Some cities have three and some have
five. Staunton has twenty-two, and they all try to run it a different way."[25]

What did the Staunton experiment represent? Many saw it as the first
city manager community in the country; with the appointment of Charles
E. Ashburner in 1908, it also had the first city manager. But the city
manager concept was already in the air. In 1899, in an editorial in
California Municipalities, Haven A. Mason, one of the founders and first
secretary of the League of California Cities had proposed the establishment of the post of "business manager" (his editorial is reproduced in
Appendix B), and Professor Charles E. Merriam of the University of
Chicago, as a member of the Chicago Charter Convention (1905–6) had
unsuccessfully advocated the idea of an appointed chief executive for
Chicago. Moreover, in 1904 Ukiah, California had created the post of chief
executive officer, to be selected by the city council (although he was not
explicitly called "manager").[26]

Council-manager government did not begin in Staunton, Virginia, but

Staunton's was the first well-documented and well-publicized case where the various trends and influences of the period—the pressure of urbanization, the popularity of business and corporate ideas, the demand for progressive reforms—combined (or perhaps collided) to produce the form of government later known as the council-manager plan. More important, Staunton, not Ukiah, California, caught the eye of Richard S. Childs, a relatively obscure figure who gave the city manager concept national prominence and popularity.

The Work of Richard S. Childs

The Staunton experiment might never have been noted had Richard Childs not surfaced at the same historical moment to develop and refine the idea. It may well be one of those peculiar accidents of history that the right man was in the right place at the right time. One can only speculate about what would have happened if he had not been there. Undoubtedly, as this writer has argued, the ideological and social forces already existed to make appointed executive government a reality, and it was a reality in places like Ukiah, California and Staunton, Virginia.

Then what did Richard Childs do for the manager concept? Why was he so important for its development? Richard Childs was the quintessential Progressive reformer—a man of means, with a social conscience, a professional background, and extra time to devote to his pet hobby, municipal reform.[27] Born in 1882, Childs grew up in a prosperous New York business family (his father was president of the Bon Ami Company) and graduated from Yale in 1904.[28] After graduation he embarked on an advertising career, but reform soon became his avocation. In 1909, with the support of Woodrow Wilson, the president of Princeton University, and James Bryce, then British ambassador to the United States, Childs founded the Short Ballot Organization, which campaigned for the reduction of the long voting lists on the ballot as a way to eliminate the corrupt political influence of the party bosses. The Short Ballot Organization also supported commission government, which had originated eight years before in Galveston, Texas.

Nevertheless, the commission plan had several shortcomings which Childs and other reformers were unhappy with. First, the electorate rarely selected the ablest administrators as commissioners. Capable professional people often were reluctant to enter the political arena, and when they did, they were frequently beaten by the political pros. In addition, administrative confusion and inefficiency were widespread in commission government. The equality of the five elected commissioners often provided no central direction; in many cases they seemed to be only individual department heads, making their own policies separately.

In a fascinating letter to Lawrence M. Conant, associate editor of *World's Work*, dated May 1, 1931, Childs explained how he developed the council-manager plan in order to correct the shortcomings of commission government:

> Shortly after I saw your article on Staunton, I conceived the idea that the city manager feature united to the commission plan would provide a new plan analogous to the business corporation and to the German burgomaster set-up, which would be very much superior to the commission plan, which, at that time was coming rapidly into vogue and bringing with it some advantages as well as some serious defects of organization.
>
> I was then a volunteer secretary of the National Short Ballot Organization, which I had organized in 1909, with Woodrow Wilson, as President. I was also secretary of the New York Short Ballot Organization, whose mission was to push for the application of our short ballot ideas in the State of New York. In the latter capacity, I laid out a program for an optional municipal government law, which would make the commission plan available to all the smaller cities of the state, in a form ready for adoption by referendum. I twisted the standard commission form to provide for a city manager and an elaborate bill was drafted by my assistant, H. S. Gilbertson.
>
> I did this without consulting the governing board of the New York Short Ballot Organization and brought the bill to them as a finished piece of work for their endorsement. They declined to endorse it for publication, as part of the association's program, preferring to keep the simpler strategy of trying to get the minor state officers made appointive—one task at a time, so the bill was left on our hands. Looking around then for someone to father it, we got it sponsored by the Lockport Board of Trade, which introduced it in the legislature. The National Short Ballot Organization, forthwith, gave it generous publicity in its press releases; secured for it the attention of charter commissions all over the country; Woodrow Wilson mentioned it in one of his speeches on a western tour; it was put into a technical book that we published for the aid of charter commissions—Beard's *Loose-Leaf Digest of Short Ballot Charters;* papers on the "Lockport Plan" were gotten into various civic conventions and magazines; and thus the idea was put on the map in a campaign which went on for ten years under my personal and enthusiastic direction.[29]

Childs later concluded that his major contribution was as "the minister who performed the marriage ceremony between the city-manager plan as first thought of in Staunton and the commission plan in Des Moines," but Don K. Price has argued that he was more "a manipulator of symbols":

Mr. Childs' principal contribution was not the invention of new symbols. Most of the original symbols of the city manager plan had already been used by the advocates of commission government. What Childs did was to add substance to the symbols, by proposing a structural change in conformity with the essential spirit of commission government, which its advocates said was "just like a corporation with its board of directors." Mr. Childs saw that this "catch phrase has converted whole cities," but remarked that the commission would not be like a board of directors until it would "appoint a manager. . . ."[30]

In part Childs succeeded in playing the roles both of "minister" and of "manipulator of symbols"; more basic, however, is the fact that he was a Progressive reformer at heart. His purpose was not merely the application of business and corporate symbols to city government but rather the persistent advocacy of an alternative to what he viewed as corrupt political rule in many cities. "Democracy," he contended once, "is my prime objective and not money saving and greater efficiency. The object is to make the democratic process genuinely democratic. . . ."[31] Business symbols were a means of achieving more democracy in local government (Childs once even proposed creating a special field of study, "Democratics"). He had already campaigned for the short ballot in order to simplify the voting process and thereby enable the rational voter to choose the best candidates. Similarly his appeal for manager government was based on the belief that man is good but community institutions are corrupt; ergo, reform the evil institutions with the technique of manager government so that the "good" can govern.

Childs's twentieth-century American Progressive thinking was a close relative of Rousseau's eighteenth-century romanticism. Both men saw an essential goodness and rationality in man. Both were convinced of the need to make government more responsive to the popular will through institutional reform—only Childs used business metaphors instead of "the General Will." "The difficulties of democracy," wrote Childs, "are mechanistic, not moral, and respond to mechanistic corrections. . . . It is the mechanism that makes the difference."[32] With that optimistic and rational view of the universe, Childs campaigned throughout his life for numerous mechanical devices to improve local democracy: short ballots, manager government, nonpartisanship, to name a few. In his book *Civic Victories,* he even postulated three universal and unassailable principles for any form of government: "elective offices must be visible," "the constituency must be wieldy," and "governments must be well integrated."[33] Rousseau and Jefferson would certainly feel at home with Childs's faith in the rationality of man, the virtue of humanity, and the benefits of local autonomy.

In *The Liberal Tradition in America,* Louis Hartz identifies the romantic core of Progressive thought, of which Childs was one of the best representatives:

> It does not take a deep analyst to see that the whole issue of "direct government," that passionate symbol of the Progressive days, was involved root and branch in the problem [of equality]. Why smash bosses and elect Senators directly? . . . The answer was: to give every last individual an equal chance to govern, and if you throw in the initiative, referendum, recall and short ballot you give him a chance to govern in practically every situation. Here was the equality of the Horatio Alger world flowering into politics. . . .[34]

Richard Childs worked especially hard between 1910 and 1920 in promoting "the equality of the Horatio Alger world" through the technique of manager government. He wrote out the first council-manager plan in 1910 for the board of trade of Lockport, New York to sponsor for adoption as the city charter. Although the New York legislature failed to pass legislation allowing Lockport to adopt the plan, Childs generated considerable press coverage in the process, so that numerous towns across the country began adopting it. First, Sumter, South Carolina, then Dayton, Ohio, and by 1918 nearly a hundred communities could boast of having "the most modern form of municipal government."

Childs did this all from his New York City Short Ballot office, often without knowing where or how his publicity was being used. As John Porter East noted:

> Childs . . . played no specific role in the Sumter victory until after the South Carolina legislature had approved the plan and the people of Sumter had accepted it by referendum. In brief, his materials were used extensively in that crusade, but he was unaware that they were being used and he played no personal part. After acceptance of the plan, Childs did assist the new council in the preparation of an advertisement for a manager. . . .[35]

Along with crystallizing the manager concept in popular form and giving it national publicity, Childs also succeeded in gaining institutional and academic acceptance for his plan. The specific institution was the National Municipal League whose Standing Committee on Commission Government contained a number of the prominent scholars of the era, including William Bennett Munro of Harvard University, Charles A. Beard of Columbia University, Ernest S. Bradford, author of a history of commission government, and Clinton Rogers Woodruff, the league's secretary. In 1898 the league had supported the "strong-mayor" form of government in its Model City Charter. In 1911 its Committee on Commission Government reported that the commission plan "had brought about democratic control of municipal government through unification of powers." A year later, however, Childs became a member of the committee, and, as Alfred Willoughby has written:

> By 1913, influenced by the Lockport Plan . . . and by Childs, the committee, at the League's Toronto conference, switched its approval to the commission-manager idea. Accordingly, a reactivated Committee on Municipal Program was instructed to draft a new Model City Charter that prescribed the commission-manager form of government. At the 1915 conference, held in Dayton, the first large city to adopt the manager plan, this innovation was approved.[36]

Willoughby gives the credit for the adoption of the new Model City Charter to the Young Turks, young men in their twenties and thirties like Lent D. Upson of Detroit and Frederick P. Gruenberg of Philadelphia who were led by Richard Childs and who persuaded the older men in the league—Charles E. Merriam, A. Lawrence Lowell, Frank J. Goodnow, and A. R. Hutton—to endorse the council-manager idea. The Young Turks also succeeded in having the league sponsor an active national education campaign for the plan.

In 1915 Richard Childs won his case for the manager concept: the National Municipal League adopted it as part of its reform package in the Model City Charter. Although the league's Charter was revised in 1925, 1933, 1941, and 1964, the manager concept has remained its central program, unchanged since 1915. Its adoption as the official program of the National Municipal League, coupled with the support of the eminent scholars of the period, gave the manager concept a sudden and dramatic national appeal. One indication of the blossoming interest in the idea was the flood of new books and periodicals that soon appeared hotly favoring the manager plan: Harry Toulmin, *The City Manager* (1915); Herman G. James, *What is the City Manager Plan?* (1917); Tso-Shuen Chang, *History and Analysis of the Commission and City Manager Plans of Municipal Government in the United States* (1918); Charles E. Mabie, ed., *The City Manager Plan of Government* (1918), and Chester E. Rightor, *The City Manager in Dayton* (1919).

The Spread of the Council-Manager Plan

Although Childs found time now and then to write articles and give speeches favoring the manager idea, most of his energies were directed toward running the family firm, the Bon Ami Company, and later toward his position as executive vice-president of Lederle Laboratories (from which he retired in 1944). But even without his central direction the plan made spectacular growth.

The council-manager plan underwent its greatest growth during two periods: the post–World War I decade, when the number of manager cities quadrupled (from one hundred to four hundred cities), and the post–World War II decades, when again the number nearly quadrupled (from six hundred to twenty-two hundred cities). Why has the manager concept gained such wide acceptance and popularity? Specifically, why has it prospered in the postwar decades?

The Post–World War I Decade: The Cult of Efficiency

Slogans like "More Business in Government," "Economy and Efficiency," "Less Government," were common during the 1920s. The era saw the first introduction of the methods of scientific management in government in order to reduce costs, improve efficiency, and eliminate dishonesty. Systematic budgeting and accounting methods were adopted at the federal level for the first time, based on the recommendations of the Taft Commission on Economy and Efficiency. Also personnel management—personnel training, merit classifications, efficiency ratings— was applied to government, and although the civil service system had existed since the 1880s, it was extended and refined by legislation like the Rogers Act, which established the diplomatic corps in 1924.

The 1920s witnessed an outpouring of innovative ideas on public administration by many of its founding fathers, among them White, Willoughby, Bruere, Cleveland, Gulick, Beard, and William E. Mosher. Commenting on the administrative thought of this era, Frederick C. Mosher notes that the period was deeply "dedicated to growth and progress; . . . a philosophy of rationality; and . . . a faith in science and scientific method and its applicability to the practical lives of men and women; a reawakening of Auguste Comte's positivism." In short, efficient administration was good; inefficient administration was bad.[37]

The spirit of the post–World War I decade was ideally suited to the development of the manager plan. The corporate and business appearance of the plan made it an attractive political idea, as Harold A. Stone, Don K. Price, and Kathryn H. Stone emphasize:

> Perhaps the most popular argument in favor of the city manager plan was the analogy of the business corporation. The similarity between municipal government and business had been observed before the invention of the city manager plan; it had been an argument for nonpartisan government in general and for the commission plan in particular. But advocates of the city manager plan were able to point out the similarity between the position of the city manager and that of the general manager of a large corporation.

Especially during the 1920's, when "more business in government" was a weighty appeal, this analogy had tremendous influence.[38]

The *Dallas News,* which during the 1920s conducted one of the most thorough and intelligent campaigns for council-manager government, summed up its arguments this way:

> Why not run Dallas itself on a business schedule by business methods under businessmen? . . . the city manager plan is after all only a business management plan. . . . The city manager is the executive of a corporation under a board of directors. Dallas is the corporation. It is as simple as that. Vote for it.[39]

In short, the *News* editorial arguments ran, with businessmen and business methods installed in city hall, government would become nonpolitical and, therefore, economical, and—although this was not expressly stated—an economical government might very well reduce taxes. Frequently mingled with a call for economy and efficiency in government was the equally persuasive appeal for civic progress, as another quotation from the *Dallas News* points up: "Dallas is now at the parting of the ways. It can remain in the small city class or go up into the big city class."[40]

Using the twin themes of "business methods" and "civic progress," local chapters of the United States Chamber of Commerce distributed to their members a report, *The City Manager Plan of Municipal Government,* that stressed the advantages of the manager plan as a modern approach in lowering taxes and eliminating politics from city government. A similar publication, *The Story of the City Manager Plan: The Most Democratic and Efficient Form of Municipal Government,* issued by the National Municipal League, appealed to identical ideas.[41]

Behind the rhetoric, nevertheless, there were often new community programs and projects that really did need efficient administration. These projects varied from city to city. In Staunton, Virginia, the demands for better roads helped to create a need for the specialized expertise of a city manager. Similarly, across the nation in the 1920s towns and cities were experiencing the shocks of urbanization. Automobiles, airplanes, electricity, new water and sewer facilities presented complex technical problems that the elected officials were often unable or unwilling to deal with. Councilmen were in many instances eager to turn these projects over to full-time technicians who could relieve them of many of the administrative minutiae and details; and trained managers were doubtless better qualified to manage sewage disposal, water purification, gas production, and garbage removal.

Coupled with the ideological and pragmatic reasons for local support for manager government, there appeared to be solid commitment to the manager idea among leading members of the academic community. Many outstanding professors of the social sciences during the early 1900s were deeply involved in supporting the council-manager plan: William B. Munro and A. Lawrence Lowell of Harvard University; Leonard D. White and Charles E. Merriam, University of Chicago; Thomas H. Reed, University of Michigan; John N. Pfiffner, University of Southern California; William Anderson, University of Minnesota; and William Mosher, Syracuse University. Members of this impressive body of American scholars frequently spoke in public and wrote in favor of the manager idea. Many attended the managers' annual conventions; one prominent professor of the era, C. A. Dykstra, even served as the city manager of Cincinnati, Ohio.

Why was academic backing for the manager idea so strong? What prompted the convergence of intellectual thinking and managerial philosophy during the 1920s? One important factor was the cult of efficiency, which was popular among both academicians and managers. Both scholarly and popular opinion marched in step to the tunes of Taylorism and scientific management, the dominant symbols of the period. Many favored, to repeat Frederick Mosher, the concept that "efficient administration was 'good'; inefficient administration was 'bad.'" Convinced of this fundamental premise, Dr. A. R. Hatton of Northwestern University could praise city managers at their 1926 convention: "You managers are the exemplars of a radically different idea in municipal affairs, of the idea that intelligence and the scientific method have a place in city government. . . ."[42] Leonard White, writing on city managers during the same year, could say, "The managers have been successful in maintaining praiseworthy standards of administration. In most cities they have greatly reduced the influence of politics. . . . They have planned intelligently and executed efficiently."[43]

The Post—World War II Period: The Ideology of Suburbia

After the depression and World War II, the driving force that spawned the manager movement immediately following the First World War, namely "the cult of efficiency," was clearly on the wane. The popularity of business and corporations had faded, along with the support of most leading social scientists.[44] Nevertheless, the popularity of the manager plan continued undaunted; again, the number of manager cities nearly quadrupled over the next two decades (from six hundred to twenty-two hundred cities). What accounts for the undiminished growth of city management in the modern world?

Part of the explanation can be found in the census figures. Between 1950 and 1960 the census showed a 23.6 million population increase for the nation's metropolitan areas; in the same period, however, the major "core cities" lost population: St. Louis's population dropped by 100,000, Detroit's by 180,000, Cleveland's by 30,000, and Washington, D.C.'s by 38,000. Yet the population for these metropolitan areas showed striking gains, largely on account of suburban growth: the St. Louis area increased by 19.8 percent; the Detroit area by 24.7 percent; the Cleveland area by 22.6 percent; the Washington area by 36.7 percent. A specific case in point was New York City, which lost 109,973 people between 1950 and 1960 but whose suburban counties in the same ten years made spectacular growth: Nassau County increased by 93 percent, Rockland by 53 percent, Suffolk by 141 percent, and Westchester by 29 percent. New York City lost 1.5 percent of its total population while its suburbs grew by 75 percent. Throughout the country, core city population gained a total of 5.6 million people, an increase of 10.7 percent, compared to suburban growth, which totaled 18 million people—an increase of 48.6 percent. As Edward C. Banfield has written: "A huge pent-up demand on the part of the well-off, whose numbers had been swelled by formation of new families, wartime prosperity, and home-loan provisions of the G.I. Bill, burst forth in a mass exodus from the city to the suburbs. . . ."[45]

The expanding suburban populations created sudden new demands for public services—sewers, water, roads, schools, housing—as well as for more sorts of new local governments. Between 1950 and 1960 over 300 municipalities and over 700 special districts in metropolitan areas came into existence. By 1960 Chicago had 1,113 local units, Philadelphia, 876, Pittsburgh, 704, New York, 551, and St. Louis, 474. The situation of continually subdividing the metropolitan area led H. G. Wells to observe many years ago, ". . . The crazy quilt hodgepodge of local government appears like fifteenth century houses which have been continuously occupied by a succession of enterprising but short-sighted and close-fisted owners, and which have now been, with the very slightest use of lath and plaster partitions and geyser hot water apparatus, converted into modern residential flats."[46]

Administering the "crazy quilt hodgepodge of local government" became an intricate specialty where independent units "squabbled incessantly over jurisdictional problems: the intersection of streets at town boundaries, the acquisition of water supply, the disposal of sewage, the health nuisances which one government visited upon another; not to mention the maintenance of their own schools, their own police forces, their own fire departments."[47]

The shocks of suburbanization in the 1950s caused many councils to turn to managers for help. Coping with the new array of public facilities and intergovernmental problems became so complex that the elected officials were often unable or unwilling to deal with them. Councilmen were eager to turn these intricate problems over to a technician and relieve themselves of many of the administrative difficulties. In short, they sought someone who was a specialist at city management. Hence, a spurt in growth of manager government appeared after World War II, particularly in new suburban settlements.

Perhaps even more important than the practical reasons for its adoption was the fact that the manager plan was ideologically attractive to the suburban cast of mind. "Suburbia," as Robert Wood aptly puts it, "defined as an ideology, a faith in communities of limited size and a belief in the condition of intimacy is quite real. The dominance of the old values explains more about the people and the politics of the suburbs than any other interpretation." The older Jeffersonian grass-roots ideology that stressed the virtue of cohesive small government and small society "has remained to shape the American metropolis and make it what it is today." As Wood laments, however, "for all our changes in culture and behavior, for all the heavy price we pay in inadequate local public service, nonexistent metropolitan services and high taxes, the good life and the good government still must come for us in small packages."[48]

The suburban faith in small government fits the philosophy of manager government perfectly. The manager concept had, after all, originally been popularized by Richard Childs as an alternative to boss rule through the progressive techniques of direct government coupled with centralized "business-like government." Childs's manager plan combined the twin Progressive reform themes of grass-roots control of government and rationally administered government by neutral experts.

What sort of government could better fit suburban needs for the 1950s? Confused by the complexity of the metropolitan age and yet clinging to the Jeffersonian ideal of small communities, the suburbs frequently found that manager government answered both their modern needs: centralized administrative authority under an expert manager, combined with direct local participation in city councils. In manager governments—a Jeffersonian small government in a metropolitan age—the suburbanites, so to speak, could have their cake and eat it too. Perhaps it was an expensive government, a government that frequently failed to serve the broader metropolitan needs, but it did work and did serve the needs of the new flourishing suburban majorities, by way of both ideology and pragmatic results.

The Spin-off from the Council-Manager Plan: The CAO

The manager movement originally began, in the hands of Richard Childs, as a combination of the commission plan and the Staunton experiment. As a philosophy, the plan grew and fed on the popular ideology of the times, but it too spawned mutations. The most notable one was the idea of the Chief Administrative Officer (CAO).

The CAO idea grew out of the flirtation of large cities with the manager plan. As early as 1926 a San Francisco good government committee sponsored by the *San Francisco News* advocated the manager plan for the city, but in 1930 a large majority of the San Francisco Charter Revision Commission decisively rejected manager government. While several members of the commission strongly favored the plan, others still backed the strong-mayor form of government. As William H. Nanry wrote, ". . . the hearing indicated a necessity for a compromise between a strong mayor and manager form."[49] The resulting compromise was the creation of a new post called Chief Administrative Officer (CAO). The CAO had fewer administrative powers than the city manager, and his role was made subordinate to that of the elected mayor. As Charles Adrian commented on San Francisco's action:

> . . . the first position of CAO was established in a typical American pattern of expediency and compromise. In accordance with the reformer's distrust of politicans, the CAO was made appointive by the mayor, but could be removed only by recall or by hearings followed by a two-thirds vote of the Board of Supervisors. The San Francisco CAO was given authority over a number of departments, but he has never been given the full powers that his title implies. He is powerless so far as his overhead [staff] functions are concerned.[50]

The CAO post in the San Francisco Charter of 1931 was the first of its kind in the United States, and after World War II it was adopted by other large cities: Louisville in 1948, Philadelphia and Los Angeles in 1951, New Orleans and Hoboken in 1952, and New York, Boston, and Newark in 1953.

The CAO concept was attractive for many of those communities that wanted to retain their strong-mayor form of government while at the same time upgrading the quality of administrative and managerial skills in local government. Also the CAO idea avoided the "managerial values" which were often viewed as an unacceptable part of the council-manager plan, and therefore it fitted more comfortably into local American political life, which traditionally placed the mayor at the forefront of political leadership and party battles.

Today the mayor-appointed administrator is called by many different names such as city administrator, deputy mayor, managing director, business administrator, or administrative officer. By and large, though, whatever his title may be, the CAO is appointed by and serves at the pleasure of the mayor without a specified term. Like a city manager, the CAO is generally charged with three important duties: first, dealing with personnel matters such as hiring and firing of municipal employees; second, supervising line operations of governmental agencies; and third, serving as an important source of administrative and managerial advice to the mayor on various public policy issues. In every city, however, the responsibilities of mayor-appointed administrators vary according to the needs of the communities in which CAOs work. In Philadelphia, New Orleans, and Newark, for example, the charters give the CAO many of the same responsibilities and functions as city managers, with responsibilities for budget preparation, control over most departments, and powers over personnel selection. In other cities, such as New York, San Francisco, and Boston, the CAO serves more as a staff aide to the mayor and presides over some, not all, line functions. But even in "weak CAO" cities, this office, as Wallace Sayre and Herbert Kaufman wrote of New York City, "became the most fully realized assets of the Mayor's Office. . . . the Mayor's most active problem solver. . . ."[51]

While the CAO idea contains many qualities of adaptability that the council-manager plan does not have, Dr. Edwin O. Stene of the University of Kansas has pointed out a major shortcoming of mayor-appointed administrators: "Many of the administrators are political rather than professional assistants; and even the trained administrators come and go with political fortunes of their mayors. While no precise statistical data are available, a casual look at mayor-appointed administrators indicates that their tenure does not equal that of the average city manager, and few indeed have the opportunity to develop careers through mobility from city to city."[52] Dr. Stene sees another difficulty with mayor-appointed administrators: "Perhaps the most frustrating experiences of the mayor-appointed administrator result from the inability to submit their own recommendations to the city council. The writer recalls how two administrators reported instances in which mayors who were engaged in campaigns for election to higher offices suppressed virtually all plans prepared for submission to council, apparently out of fear that any controversial matter discussed in council would arouse political opposition rather than encourage new support."[53]

Summary

At a time when many western intellectuals were wrestling with the issues posed by Marx—class conflict and a "new social order"—American Progressives were battling for technical reforms which they believed would make American democracy more democratic. The Progressives, instead of plotting revolutions, busied themselves with promoting equality, here and there, in bits and pieces, by various formulas. One of these prominent reform ideas was the council-manager plan, a unique American hybrid of the intellectual and social forces of the Progressive era: the growth of urbanization, the popularity of business and corporate ideals, the Progressive reform movement, the scientific management and public administration movements. The major goal, as Richard Childs and other early reformers originally believed, was to rid the cities of boss rule and extend the democratic processes.

But movements and philosophies have a habit of changing, frequently through no fault of the founders (witness Marxism). This was particularly true of the manager movement. Its two periods of greatest expansion—the immediate post–World War decades—came about through two very different influences. In the 1920s the plan prospered because of the national vogue of efficiency, as well as the rising impact of urbanization that accompanied the peace and prosperity of the times. During the 1950s, in response to the postwar migration from central cities, the plan's growth shifted to suburbia, supporting suburban physical and ideological needs. In the process of growth, the manager plan even created its own philosophical offshoot, the CAO, which gained popularity in large communities.

Far from being a static doctrine, the council-manager plan has deftly adapted to the temper of the times. It originated in response to the cry for an end to boss rule, then answered the call for efficient government, and next it emerged in a second renaissance to support the suburban desire for Jeffersonian grass-roots democracy in the complex age of the metropolis. And with each "reappearing act" its "inventor," Richard Childs, has tenaciously held to the "purity of his plan." So have most of the staunch advocates of reform.[54]

2

The Development of the
City Management Profession:
The Pre–World War II Heritage

History

> The greatest achievement of American administration is the city manager.
> He is a type par excellence in public administration, marked by integrity, by
> competence and by adjustability.
>
> Charles E. Merriam
> *Public Management* (1945)

> I look upon my profession as city manager in exactly the same way that a
> minister of the gospel looks upon his mission and believe that as a city
> manager endeavoring to make the city for whose administrative affairs I am
> responsible, better in every way for every man and woman, boy and girl in
> it, I am doing on earth the work of the Master.
>
> Louis Brownlow
> ICMA Convention (1922)

Throughout the late nineteenth and early twentieth centuries most Progressive reform campaigns stressed the necessity of instituting a new system of municipal government that would eliminate the corrupt influence of political machines and boss rule. A variety of techniques were advocated by the municipal reformers to achieve this goal: the short ballot, the commission plan, at-large elections, the popular initiative, the referendum, the recall, and the merit system of personnel administration. Reform advocates saw the short ballot as a means of providing greater visibility of governmental offices; the commission plan offered a vehicle for eliminating political corruption with city administration; at-large elections ended gerrymandering of election districts; the initiative, the referendum, and the recall permitted wider direct involvement by the citizenry in political decisions; and the merit system was viewed as a device to end the spoils system. In the eyes of the reformers, the council-manager plan, as devised originally by Richard Childs and actively supported by the National Municipal League, was the most potent, perfected instrument for fighting corruption in municipalities. Here was the ideal way of stamping out the odious influence of bossism by electing a small city council at large with broad policy-making powers while vesting the day-to-day administrative responsibilities of local government in a professional city manager and his staff. Richard Childs liked to say that politics went out the window when Dayton's first city manager blew in.

Though the council-manager plan originated as part of the broader Progressive reform movement, the city management profession grew out of the needs of individual managers to share their common concerns of municipal operation and gain professional status for their new occupation. While the reformers were campaigning for "a modern form of municipal government," the managers were confronting the day-to-day practical problems and responsibilities of local government. Thus, almost from the outset, the interests and points of view of the two groups, reformers and managers, sharply diverged.

If the members of the National Municipal League searched for a means to rid cities of bosses, managers faced another kind of problem: namely, how to run their communities. Frequently the councils they served asked the managers to govern the city "efficiently" and "effectively." Sometimes the managers were successful at this task and sometimes they were not, but as city managers their primary concerns centered on institutional operation as opposed to institutional change.

This is not to imply that managers were uninterested in the advancement of the city manager movement. Managers had a considerable personal stake in the spread of the manager plan, and during the early years of the existence of the manager's association, it made frequent contact with the National Municipal League. Yet, from the beginning, it was also clear these two organizations, although sympathetic to each other's work, had fundamentally different goals. For example, the third conference of the National Municipal League (1897) set up its organizational strategy "as a platform upon which municipal campaigns should be waged,"[1] whereas the second meeting of the City Managers' Association (1915) enacted bylaws "to promote the efficiency of city managers and municipal work."[2]

This chapter will endeavor to examine three important elements of the pre–World War II manager's organization that later served to shape the basic features of the modern city manager profession: the development of its organizational structure, the character of its early members, and the substance of its professional outlook.

The Emergence of a Professional Identity: 1914–24

During the first decade of the City Managers' Association, much of what is now the present organizational structure of the profession took shape: (1)

the growth of the City Managers' Association and the establishment of its early professional boundaries; (2) its governance by committees of the professional elites; (3) the weakness of financial resources and personnel controls; (4) the creation of university educational programs in city management; and (5) the formulation of the code of ethics as a professional ideal.

The Growth of the City Managers' Association and the Establishment of Professional Boundaries

It was no coincidence that the city manager association began at the time when many other professional groups were also forming their associations. The late nineteenth and early twentieth centuries, as we saw in Chapter 1, had witnessed a sharp increase in the urban population which resulted in new demands for specialized public service occupations. A number of professional groups organized nationally and sought professional recognition for the first time during this period. Therefore, it was not strange that Henry M. Waite, himself already involved in a professional engineering society, should have initiated the first meeting of city managers shortly after becoming Dayton's first city manager, as Richard B. Vogel has described:

> Henry M. Waite, Dayton's Manager, after studying engineering at Massachusetts Institute of Technology, had established a national reputation as an engineer before his appointment; it was quite natural, therefore, that the initial impetus for the establishment of an association would come from him. Technically, Waite had made the suggestion in response to a letter written to him by the newly appointed Manager of Amarillo, Texas, H. M. Hardin. Hardin had also written to Charles Ashburner, the first city manager in the United States, then serving as the City Manager of Springfield, Ohio. Following up Waite's recommendation, a letter was sent to all 31 city managers inviting them to join in the formation of a professional association. It had been agreed that the initial meeting would be held in Springfield, Ohio, and of the 17 Managers responding to Hardin's letter, 8 were able to be present.[3]

Though enthusiastic, the first gathering, at Springfield, Ohio, was hardly an impressive event. Only one-quarter of the nation's managers attended, and the proceedings of the first meeting were reminiscent of Elks or Rotary Club conventions. For the most part the managers exchanged light remarks. For instance, asked how he handled his relationship with the city council, Manager Hardin of Amarillo, Texas replied: "I care for them to meet only once a month; that's often enough. That's to allow the monthly bills and allow the payroll to be paid." Hardin felt fortunate that he only had three councilmen to "herd" together once a month.[4]

In 1919 the City Managers' Association began publishing a monthly newsletter, *The City Manager Bulletin,* an important link with its members, which listed job openings and current professional news. A sample copy dated May 1923 had articles on "Elements of Budget Making," "Separate and Combined Sewers," "A Municipal Ice Plant," "A Citizen Advisory Committee," "A Rating Form for Policemen," and "Organization Charting."

To establish its own separate professional identity, the association had to secure its independence from the two reform organizations chiefly responsible for promoting the manager plan throughout the country: the National Municipal League and the U.S. Chamber of Commerce's American City Bureau.

The National Municipal League remains even today the major sponsor of the council-manager plan. Several managers could be found in attendance at the league's annual meetings up to 1923, and the league held regular panel discussions on the subject of manager government. But although some managers attended the league meetings, few league members were prominent participants in the managers' association. The pedestrian problems of municipal management that interested managers seemed to have little appeal to the reformers' broader political interests. Similarly, the managers tended to reject much of the large-scale theorizing of the reformers. When Richard Childs at the 1915 league conference tried to persuade the managers to adopt certain "professional and ethical standards," "Colonel Waite lost no time in casting aspersions upon theorists; Manager Cummins added that some of the unasked advice of these theorists appeared to 'us' as little more than bosh; Manager Carr hastened 'to endorse most heartily what had been said by Brother Waite and Brother Cummins.' "[5]

Childs and the members of the National Municipal League ended their influence over the subsequent development of the city manager profession with that brief encounter in 1915, even though the league continued to remain an active proponent of manager government.[6]

The influence of the U.S. Chamber of Commerce's American City Bureau was also strongly evidenced in the early development of the City Managers' Association. The American City Bureau, whose major function was planning for the growth of the individual branches of the chamber of commerce in local communities, actively supported the early manager association, as H. G. Otis described in the first issue of the *City Manager Bulletin:*

> The American City Bureau, to whose organization service the modern Chamber of Commerce is so deeply indebted, has definitely

undertaken the promotion of commission-manager government. It is equipped to furnish men to speak upon the new plan, to aid in charter drafting, to conduct publicity work and even to manage campaigns for the adoption of a manager charter.

Lucius E. Wilson, director of the Bureau's field staff, is the man who introduced the manager plan into Dayton, Ohio, and he played a leading part in the successful charter campaign in that city. Dr. A. R. Hatton, of Western Reserve University, is acknowledged as one of the country's leading charter authorities and has recently made an extended tour as field secretary of the National Short Ballot Organization, visiting the leading cities operating under the manager plan. The Bureau has contracted for a large part of his time.[7]

The bureau not only actively sponsored the manager plan throughout the country, but also paid for the full time employment of H. G. Otis as the City Managers' Association's executive secretary (1918–21), providing him with office space in New York City and supporting the early publications of the *City Manager Bulletin*. This arrangement, as Richard B. Vogel has written, benefited the chamber of commerce since "their interests were enhanced by assisting the Association, if this would increase activity on the part of the city manager towards encouraging the establishment of a Chamber of Commerce in his city if none existed already."[8] The relationship with the bureau lasted until July 1921 when Otis accepted the managership of Clarksburg, Virginia. Shortly thereafter the City Managers' Association's headquarters was moved to Kansas.

Governance by the Professional Elite

The existence of a separate City Managers' Association brought up many questions of organizational policy. These issues were regularly resolved by committees of the profession's elite. Senior managers representing a wide variety of backgrounds and communities were asked frequently to serve on *ad hoc* panels to examine and report on specific professional problems. This practice permitted representation of a broad spectrum of professional viewpoints in resolving the association's policy issues. In a sense the "elder managers," Waite, Cummins, and Carr, in the confrontation with Richard Childs at the 1915 National Municipal League Meeting, acted as this type of *ad hoc* panel representing the managers' professional point of view. Later, during the 1920s, it became standard practice for the association to appoint *ad hoc* committees to resolve their professional problems at annual conventions. Often distinguished professors were added to the panels, along with public officials, depending on the subject under discussion.

Several of the noteworthy committees that appeared (and disappeared) included: a committee "to prepare a manual of standard managerial practice" chaired by John H. Edy; "a committee on objectionable charter provisions" chaired by Ossian E. Carr; a committee "on professional research" chaired by Louis Brownlow; a committee "on the association activities and future program" chaired by Ossian E. Carr; a committee "on professional conduct" chaired by Bert C. Wells; a committee "on a code of ethics" chaired by Ossian E. Carr; and a committee "on training for city managers" chaired by Luther Gulick. The policy recommendations of several of these panels will be discussed in the following pages.

Weakness of Financial Resources and Personnel Controls

Within its first decade the City Managers' Association was able to assert its independence from the National Municipal League and the American City Bureau, yet the problem of adequate financial support continually plagued the association. The publication of a journal and periodicals, a paid staff at a national headquarters, and annual convention costs were heavy expenses for a new voluntary organization. In 1915 its total annual revenue was $105; in 1920, $3,284; and in 1924, $10,000. For the same years its expenditures were $76, $3,000, and $9,800. Virtually all its major cash income was derived from membership and advertising fees, and its expenditures largely went for publications and staff salaries. To find new revenue sources the organization opened its membership to associate and contributing members, raised its active members' dues from $5 to $15, and made occasional appeals to the general membership for greater financial support. H. G. Otis solicited the managers' help in 1921:

> Following our custom of the past two years, all members of the association are invited to cooperate in securing advertisements for our *Yearbook*. You will find enclosed letters addressed to you which you are at liberty to forward to firms whose services you have found to be satisfactory.[9]

The young association also had major difficulties in attracting membership and controlling individual managers' activities. Joining the organization and attending its meetings were purely voluntary actions. Only one-quarter of the managers attended the first convention in 1914, and in the same year only a little more than one-half of the managers took out membership. Even a decade later, only about a quarter of the membership attended the annual conventions and about one-third of the total number of managers did not belong to the organization. The managers that failed to join, Leonard White believed:

> . . . were not professional managers at all and have no general

interest in the city manager movement. A few of them are fearful of offending some local feeling by joining an outside organization (Manager Orkison of Pasadena discreetly refrains from joining the Association of which his predecessor was President).[10]

In the debate, cited earlier, between Richard Childs and Henry Waite at the 1915 National Municipal League Convention, Childs had proposed strict membership standards for the City Manager Association, depending on whether or not the city had "the official manager plan." Waite and his colleagues challenged Childs's idea as imposing too great a restriction on the development of the professional association. Instead they sought to liberalize their membership policies at their subsequent managers' conventions in order to attract new members.

The open membership policies of the organization made membership easy to obtain and provided little cohesiveness to the new profession. Local control over hiring and firing of city managers was simply a basic part of council-manager government, and the association made no attempt to influence the employment pattern of its members, nor did it give them any career protection (unlike the American Association of University Professors or the American Bar Association). If managers lost their jobs, they were expected to fend for themselves in finding new ones. This situation led City Manager E. A. Beck, chairman of the association's Constitution Revision Committee, to observe in 1924: "As you all know, the mortality in the profession has been high. At times there have been a number of drifters in and out of the Association."[11]

Furthermore, the association had no means to discipline any of its members who exhibited unprofessional conduct (unlike the American Medical Association or the American Bar Association). The strategy was to encourage membership in every way, and although Article 6 of its 1920 constitution did not permit a member who exhibited professional "incompetency" to retain his status, the executive board made no effort to enforce or even define such standards of competence. Leonard White, writing in 1927, held that "the managers have shown no interest in such a study of their failures."[12]

The Creation of University Educational Programs in City Management

While the city management profession was weak in the realms of finances and personnel controls, it gained substantial cooperation from a number of leading academic institutions in providing professional education for city managers. The University of Michigan established an educational program in 1914; Stanford University, in 1919; the University of Southern California, in 1921; Texas A. & M., in 1924; and Syracuse

University, in 1924 (the Syracuse program began in 1911 in New York City at the Training School for Public Administration, as part of the New York Bureau of Municipal Research, and in 1924 the program was moved to Syracuse). Although these institutions developed courses in management, by the mid-1920s only three of them had actually graduated any candidates. The University of Michigan had graduated thirty-five; Texas A. & M., thirteen, and Syracuse, twenty. And of the graduates of these schools, only nine were actually serving as city managers in the mid-1920s: five from Michigan, two from Texas A. & M., and two from Syracuse. Out of a total of 340 city managers at that time, less than 3 percent had been specifically trained in city management. The rest came from a variety of different disciplines and occupations.[13]

The curricula of these schools had a distinct "functional orientation" which stressed practical courses in city administration. Syracuse, for example, offered a one-year program with courses on: "Types of Municipal Organization," "Civil Service and Personnel Management," "Budgets and Budget Making," "Public Safety and Welfare," "Street Construction and Maintenance," "Sewer Construction and Maintenance," "Waste Collection and Disposal." Combined with classroom studies there was a required three-to-six-month fieldwork internship at the Rochester Bureau of Municipal Research or in one of the several departments of New York City government.

In addition to the special programs established for training city managers, many larger universities with strong departments of political science offered courses in public administration, frequently for educating city managers. In the 1920s, the University of Cincinnati, located in one of the early manager cities, initiated courses in public administration as part of its broader program of political science. The city manager and members of his staff were hired as part-time lecturers, and the students in the program were expected to work in Cincinnati city government to supplement their classroom training.

In addition to the regular university programs in public administration, the Institute of Public Administration in New York City beginning in 1921 offered correspondence and in-service training programs for city managers (this program was later transferred to the Maxwell School, Syracuse University, and during the 1930s the ICMA took charge of the correspondence program). These in-service training programs were offered to managers and public administrators in a variety of subjects, including public works, municipal finance, city planning, police administration, fire administration, personnel administration, budgeting, municipal law, accounting, property assessment, public welfare administration, and techniques of municipal management. Summing up the ideal preparation for city managers during this period, Orin Nolting and Clarence Ridley wrote:

> . . . it is essential that they become acquainted with the tools and
> techniques of administration. For example, in personnel administra-
> tion, all the procedures from recruitment to separation from the
> service should be carefully studied. . . .[14]

In spite of their shortcomings these initial university programs symbolized the dedication of many teachers and scholars of that era to the
development of professional local administration. No reference to these
early public service programs could be complete without citing the names
of Charles A. Beard of Columbia University, William E. Mosher of the
Maxwell School, Syracuse University, and Thomas H. Reed of the
University of Michigan, who fathered the university training programs at
their respective institutions. They were persistent advocates within the
traditional academic community for university education for public
servants at a time when functional courses in administration were regarded
as unworthy of university teaching. In the day-to-day world of city
administration, these same scholars continually sought places for their
graduates to begin their careers. Often it was very difficult finding such
openings, as Thomas Reed pointed out at an annual conference of city
managers:

> Of course it is easier to find jobs for apprentices if you do not ask a
> salary for them. But most of the young men who finish a graduate
> course in municipal administration are not in a position to finance
> another year of their education. A great many of them have worked
> their way through or are going through with the help of a
> scholarship. They come to the point where they have to have at least
> a bare subsistence.[15]

The 1924 Code of Ethics as a Professional Ideal

The climax of the first decade's drive for a separate professional identity
for city managers was perhaps symbolized by the adoption of the 1924
Code of Ethics (included in Appendix C). During the early 1920s a number
of other professional groups had adopted codes of ethics. In Volume 51 of
the *Annals of the American Academy* (May 1922), several professional
codes were printed and discussed.[16] The Code of Ethics for Engineers, for
example, contained ten points that urged all engineers to conduct
themselves responsibly and "to render effective service to humanity."[17]
Whether the publication of that volume and the actions of other
professional groups influenced the managers' decision to adopt a code is
not clear. But within a year of its publication several managers began to
urge the City Managers' Association to adopt a code that would both

define the proper role of a manager in a community and establish standards for his conduct.

Both C. A. Bingham of Lima, Ohio and F. D. Danielson of Hinsdale, Illinois initiated discussions for the development of a managers' code, and in 1924 a committee of senior city managers was appointed to develop a code, chaired by Ossian E. Carr, the first president of the City Managers' Association and then manager of Fort Worth, Texas. The committee members were C. Wellington Koiner, Pasadena, California; Louis Brownlow, Knoxville, Tennessee, then president of the association; and Frank D. Danielson. Unfortunately, no record of the committee discussions exists, and the code they recommended was adopted without formal debate at the September 1924 managers' conference in Montreal, Canada.[18]

In general, the thirteen-point code reflects the spirit of professionalism with which the Association sought to identify itself. The first sentence emphasized the principal reason for the code's adoption, "in order that city managers might maintain a high standard of professional conduct." In the short paragraphs that followed the new code summarized the "ideal" behavior pattern for managers: "in personal conduct a City Manager should be exemplary"; "the City Manager is the administrator for all the people and . . . he should serve without discrimination"; "a City Manager should deal frankly with the council"; "a City Manager will be known by his works." The code reflected, as Leonard White observed, "a notably high standard of official conduct, such a standard as has never been formulated by any other analogous group of American city executives."[19]

White's comment is pertinent, for the code should not be taken too literally but rather as a general expression of the ethical ideals of the new association.[20] The managers sought to look and act like a profession even though they had not yet attained all the formal attributes of the more traditional professional callings of law or medicine. As Manager Frank Danielson argued in the pages of the *City Manager Magazine*: "A profession requires an ethical code in order that there might be a standard for the very best relations with employer, citizen, public at large, such as the other professional fraternities have to foster. . . ."[21] Or, as Louis Brownlow wrote several years afterward:

> . . . the city managers in recognizing themselves as constituting a new profession of public administrators have given to the idea of the appointive executive entrusted with administrative duties a new meaning and dignity. They represent in their professional capacity a determination to keep the technical services of local government "out of politics," and a deliberate intention to consider the problems of municipal government as being problems of a national rather than a parochial character.[22]

In keeping with this new professional philosophy, Brownlow and other members of the executive board during the early 1920s fostered several reforms in the City Managers' Association. In 1923 a permanent national headquarters for the association was established at the University of Kansas, Lawrence, Kansas, and John Stutz was hired as the full-time executive secretary. Under Stutz's direction the mimeographed *City Manager Bulletin* became the more impressive monthly *City Manager Magazine.* In 1924, a constitutional revision broadened the scope of the organization's identity by adopting a new name: the International City Managers' Association (ICMA).[23] Article 8, adopted that year, specified for the first time an explicit means of expelling members: "On the written request of ten or more active members setting forth a just cause, any member of this Association may be expelled."[24]

Summarizing the association's drive for professional recognition, Louis Brownlow, then president of the City Managers' Association, wrote in a significant editorial in the *City Manager Magazine* (1923):

> . . . I believe that the Association should leave to others the business of political propaganda, although willingly making available to all who inquire all information that we are able to procure as to the progress of the City Manager Form of Government. In the next place I believe that the Association, while furnishing information concerning openings for city managers and the names of men who desire to become city managers to interested inquirers, should completely divest itself of any semblance of an employment agency. And again, and I will say no more at this time, I believe that in our publications we should endeavor to present articles that will be of material assistance to each other in our chief and only business of improving municipal administration, leaving to others, if others deem it worthwhile, the retailing of gossip concerning those who for one cause or another don't like us.
>
> In other words, we assume as we enter upon our tenth year that our profession is an established profession, that our Association is a professional society and that our chief interest is in the work we are doing for mankind.[25]

The Early City Managers: The Pioneers of the New Profession

Were the early city managers an identifiable social group? Could they be characterized as distinctive in any way? Did they possess a unique habit of thought or professional *Weltanschauung?* Several statistical surveys of managers taken during the 1920s and 1930s showed city managers as a group tending to possess several distinctive traits.[26] For the most part they were white, native-born, American males who lived and worked in midwestern or southern communities with populations of fewer than fifty thousand (approximately three-quarters of manager communities were located in the South or Midwest in 1930; of these cities, 93 percent were under fifty thousand in population and 40 percent were under five thousand in population). The typical city manager had graduated from high school and attended college. Slightly more than half had obtained B.A. degrees and about one-tenth held advanced graduate degrees. This meant that the group was well educated, since during this period more than half of the adult American population had never attended high school. Three-fourths of those with B.A.'s studied engineering. Less than 3 percent had majored in political science or public administration.

Although most had been trained in engineering, their early occupational interests tended to be in governmental work. More than half had held various positions in government before becoming city managers, serving as department heads, city or county engineers, public utility managers, highway superintendents, city clerks, or finance officers. Other managers were drawn from a wide spectrum of private occupations: business, law, teaching, real estate, banking. At the time of his first appointment as city manager, the early manager was likely to be holding a public position, normally was in his mid-thirties, and if he was appointed before the depression, he had probably not lived previously in the city he managed (in 1933 only 19 percent of those appointed as city managers were classified as "out-of-town" men, compared to 57 percent of those appointed in 1929).[27]

By 1930 the average manager had served in his position for four years, was married, and was a man in his mid-forties. He was a member of the ICMA and read its journal, *Public Management,* but was unable to attend the association's annual conferences. (In 1930 three-fourths of the managers were members of the ICMA, but only between one-fourth and one-third of the members went to the annual meetings.) He was also a member of one or two local civic clubs like the Rotary, Lions, or chamber of commerce. He regularly subscribed to two other journals of engineering or good government. He rarely read any of the theoretical social science journals like the *American Political Science Review* or the *Annals of the American Academy of Political and Social Science.*[28]

During the 1920s his paycheck had increased by about two hundred dollars per year, and in 1929 he drew an average income of fifty-one hundred dollars, slightly better than the national average family income at that time of forty-two hundred dollars.[29] During the depths of the depression in 1933 his salary was cut by nearly one-third of what it had been in 1929.

Managers tended to put in long hours at their work, frequently ten to twelve hours over a five-and-a-half- or six-day work week. Surveys showed that their occupational world was largely confined to municipal administration. Normally, one-third of the working day was concerned with speaking to department heads, interviewing callers, and attending meetings. A quarter of the day was spent directly supervising, coordinating, and inspecting municipal activities, and an equal amount of the time was spent on planning future work. The rest of the day was taken up with miscellaneous activities such as handling correspondence.

A manager who left his post (there was approximately a 10 percent annual turnover rate among managers) was likely to go into another city management position or another public service position. During the depression many managers began entering the federal government.

In summary, the city management profession during the 1920s and 1930s tended to be a fluid but highly homogeneous group of individuals: white, male, native-born Americans, middle-class, middle-aged, college educated, residing in small or medium-sized midwestern or southern communities, and devoted to a full-time occupational specialty of municipal administration.

What were the common values or occupational perspectives exhibited by this group of public professionals? What was, so to speak, their professional *Weltanschauung?* What habits of thought gave managers a distinctive outlook on the world? In short, what were the qualities that characterized the mind of the early city manager?

Above all else, managers liked to view themselves as eminently practical men who were devoted to "getting the job done." "By God, I go into a town to build; when I can't build, I get out!" Charles E. Ashburner, the first city manager of Staunton, Virginia, told an interviewer.[30] Henry Oyen described Ashburner in *World's Work* as ". . . medium sized and twitching with nervous energy that makes the enthusiast. . . . His strongest characteristics probably are his desire for 'doing the right job.' "[31]

In his descriptions of a number of the early managers, Leonard White draws a vigorous image of the city manager as a man who likes to do things. As he wrote of Walke Truxton of Norfolk, Virginia:

> He is the personification of nervous force. He speaks rapidly and forcefully, one fist ready at any instant to pound the desk. He seems to muster all the energy of his being for constant employment at whatever matter of business may come up before him. He is an untiring worker, and is sometimes at his desk at five o'clock in the morning.

Their proudest accomplishments were the tangible changes that occurred under their administrations. White spoke admiringly of the work of C. Wellington Koiner, manager of Pasadena, California:

> A new and much needed street program was worked out, involving important extensions and some widening. Elaborate street lighting fixtures were installed. The police and fire departments were enlarged, keeping pace with the growth of the city. City planning engineers were brought from Chicago to work out a great civic center. They prepared a city plan. . . .[32]

Managers undertook practical improvements like these, however, not simply at random, but frequently out of an impulse to bring "new rationality" and "order" to the affairs of municipalities. Budgets, city planning, and a merit system were several of the tools the early managers used to impose rationality. As Thomas Reed, forty years later, summarized his work as the first city manager of San Jose, California in 1916 (see Appendix C for the full text):

> There was never a dull moment in Prunedom [San Jose at that time considered itself the prune capital of the world] while I was manager. I do not suggest that I was ideally suited for the herculean task before me. I was young, inexperienced, impulsive, hot tempered. . . .
> However, we did install a good encumbrance-type accounting system, institute carefully prepared budgets, carry on centralized purchasing with fair opportunities for competition, set up a civil service commission and a city planning commission and support a full time professional health office, acquire a competent city engineer, filter and heat the swimming pool water, and reorganize the police department under an experienced and honest chief of police.[33]

This insistence on rationality in municipal administration often brought the managers into conflict with the partisan forces that saw politics as based on personal influence rather than "merit principles." The colorful career of Ossian E. Carr offers a good case in point. Carr's career as manager consisted of one fight after another with individuals and groups who sought exceptions to his imposed rules of administrative rationality. As manager of Niagara Falls, New York, Carr fought what he termed "a corrupt vice ring" operating in city hall, which sought first to sue him and then to get rid of him by threats of death, but he stood his ground for "merit principles of personnel recruitment" and quite proudly eliminated the vice ring's influence on the hiring practices of the city. In Dubuque, Iowa, Carr broke up a similar sort of "contractors' ring" that sought "special purchasing privileges" in municipal government. Here again he won his case, though not without lengthy court battles. Then, as manager of Fort Worth, Texas, he encountered the Ku Klux Klan, which wanted special appointments for its members in city hall. The Klan burned crosses on Carr's lawn as well as on those of his neighbors, but Carr again fought for the "merit principle of hiring" and in the end won.

In addition to the pragmatic and rational temper of mind reflected in the activities of the early managers, there was also another salient characteristic in their work—a concern for ethical and responsible action. As Ossian Carr himself described early managers:

> . . . We were men upon whose shoulders fell responsibility for good government and good morals, for development and proper growth, for settling immense problems for the cities we served. We had, to put it mildly, a large sense of the community's need of us and of what we individually contributed to our various communities.[34]

This sense of responsibility for their communities led to a continuous search for the "proper principles," the "best technique," the "fundamental law" upon which to base their public actions. They could not trust the changing winds of popular sentiment to be a worthy guide for their actions. More often, they looked within themselves, to their own best judgment, for a criterion for action on policy matters affecting city administration.

As John Edy, manager of Berkeley, California, told the ICMA Convention in 1925:

> The City Manager, while endeavoring conscientiously to follow the broad policy laid down by the council, can never afford to bend his decision or recommendations to please individual members. His assumption must be that he pleases his council most when he gives it his honest and independent judgment.[35]

Following this statement, Edy enumerated fifty-one basic principles of "managerial practice in Berkeley" and urged other managers to write out "their principles of city management" and "meditate on them" for several minutes every day. Probably few managers followed Edy's advice, but the search for the best techniques of municipal administration remained a perennial topic of discussion at annual manager conventions.[36]

Along with managerial principles, there was also frequent emphasis on establishing a clear legal definition of the manager's duties in the city charter. Managers, in general, sought charters that sharply distinguished their administrative powers from the council's legislative powers. However, in their efforts to split administrative from legislative powers, managers also frequently wanted as broad a definition of their administrative roles as possible, including such powers as appointment and removal of all department heads, enforcement of all municipal laws, responsibility for budget preparation, control over all departments, and the right to sit in on council meetings without a vote. The perennial discussions at manager conventions on the topic of manager-council relationships reflected this contradictory tendency among managers to seek hard and fast legal divisions between their own administrative roles and the legislative powers of council while at the same time demanding broad administrative authority.[37]

In his continual search for proper principles, the best technique, the ideal charter and administrative law, the city manager represented an American type which David Riesman's *Lonely Crowd* has characterized as the "inner-directed" personality. The inner-directed person strives to respond to an internal code of morality, as opposed to the outer-directed individual, who responds primarily to the demands of others.[38] A typical politician might be outer-directed, continually taking his cues for action from those around him, but under Riesman's classification the city manager's personality structure would be more akin to the inner-directed personality—one that looks to its own ethical judgments as a standard for action rather than following the dictates of a peer group. No doubt it was this voice of inner direction that made many of the early managers —Ashburner, Carr, Reed, Edy, Brownlow, and Walke—appear to be driven men who pushed themselves sometimes to the point of physical exhaustion in pursuing their ideals of civic change and community improvement. Much like the seventeenth-century Puritans, the early city managers felt the heavy burden of a personal conscience pushing them to do good.

The Flowering of the Scientific Management Philosophy as the City Manager's Professional Ideology: 1925–38

During the first decade (1914–24) of the existence of the City Managers' Association, the manager's basic professional identity had taken shape. Although the new profession suffered from inadequate financial resources and legal controls over its membership, during this era the association had marked out its professional boundaries by defining its membership standards, established a pattern of having its policies set by members of the professional elite, set up links with the university community for training, recruitment, and research purposes, and crystallized its professional ideals in its 1924 Code of Ethics. By the mid-1920s, the ICMA had become much stronger and more effective than it had been in 1914. Now, instead of consisting of 17 members, it could boast 462, with a national headquarters in Lawrence, Kansas, a full-time executive staff, and a monthly journal of impressive size and scholarly content.

But with all this development, somehow, many of the organization's members believed that city management still lacked a basic prerequisite of being a profession, namely, a defined body of knowledge of universally applicable principles of city management to which every member of the profession could adhere in all situations. If the managers were to be experts at municipal management, their arguments ran, the management philosophy must in some way be codified and summarized and thus achieve the distinction of a universal science. When these principles were established, it would not be "man, nor caprice, nor will" that ruled; it would be "the System."[39]

The absence of such principles led Leonard White in 1927 to lament:

> Management as an art has been adequately portrayed in recent books, but management under the special terms and conditions of the council-manager plan has never been systematically set forth. The profession of city management urgently requires such a systematic presentation.[40]

White challenged the city managers to systematize their principles in a standard manual of city management practice. With the help of the academic world and major philanthropic foundations, over the next several years the ICMA undertook a major effort to develop the scientific management philosophy, or Taylorism, with specific application to municipal government.

Institutional and Academic Support for Taylorism

The early twentieth century saw the rise of numerous philanthropic foundations endowed by wealthy American entrepreneurs—Carnegie, Ford, Rockefeller. These men for various reasons established foundations and funds to study and improve the social and cultural life of America. One of the earliest manifestations of this philanthropic concern was the creation of organizations related to community research. A leading example of this type of organization was the New York Bureau of Municipal Research. Barry Karl describes it:

> The New York Bureau of Municipal Research had been founded in 1906, the first organization designed as a bureau of research, yet part of a continuing stream of older organizations, all dedicated to reform. The transition from reform to research was clearer in this instance, perhaps, than in any other. The founder of the Bureau was Robert Fulton Cutting, who as President of the Board of the Citizen's Union, had for many years been active in municipal reform groups of New York. Mr. Cutting, a man of wealth and family, prevailed upon his acquaintances, John D. Rockefeller and Andrew Carnegie, to join

him in providing funds for the continuation of the Bureau which he had begun as an experiment in the Citizen's Union.[41]

As Karl notes, the establishment of the bureau marked an important shift in focus from support of local reform efforts to undertaking community research into the pressing social and urban problems of the day. Characteristic of this research focus was the Laura Spelman Rockefeller Memorial Fund, established in 1918 in memory of John D. Rockefeller's wife and designated to continue her work with children and interracial relations. This fund came under the direction of Beardsley Ruml, a close friend of Charles Merriam, the distinguished professor of social science at the University of Chicago. Merriam was instrumental in encouraging Ruml to take an active interest in supporting social science research in general and public administration in particular. In 1924 Ruml and the executive board of the Spelman Fund provided the initial support for establishing the Social Science Research Council at Chicago to aid research scholarship in the social sciences. During the same period, Ruml helped to finance the National Institute of Public Administration under the direction of Charles Beard in New York City. In 1928 the Spelman Fund was merged into the present Rockefeller Foundation, but Ruml remained the head of its subdivision, the Spelman Fund of New York.[42]

Charles Merriam's connections extended to other funds as well. When he ran for mayor of Chicago in 1911 on a reform ticket, one of Merriam's chief financial backers and close friends was Julius Rosenwald, a prominent Chicago businessman. At his death Rosenwald left monies to the University of Chicago for urban research. Merriam had access to these funds for social science research activities.[43]

During the 1920s, meanwhile, pressures began building up in the International City Managers' Association to conduct a vigorous research program and expand general operations. John Stutz ultimately was replaced as the association's national executive secretary principally because of his failure to attract research funding and expand the organization's activities.[44]

Although by 1928 Louis Brownlow was no longer president of the ICMA, he continued to play an active part in developing support for the organization, and he invited his friends Charles Merriam and Beardsley Ruml to the 1928 ICMA Conference where he had been asked to talk on community planning. As Brownlow explained in his autobiography:

> In the Autumn of 1928 I went to the City Managers' Association convention in Asheville, North Carolina, there to give my illustrated lecture about Radburn and to renew my acquaintance and friendships among the city managers. I persuaded Mr. Ruml and Dr. Merriam to attend the meeting in hope that it might be possible for

the Spelman Fund to find a way to make a grant to the City Managers' Association for the improvement of its headquarters. Such a grant already had been made to a municipal administrative service, which was operated in connection with the National Municipal League and had on its board one or two city managers and local officials.[45]

This trip to the Asheville conference brought about a commitment on the part of Merriam and Ruml to further the association's activities through the resources at their disposal. At first Merriam tapped the Rosenwald Funds (with an initial grant of $10,000 per year over a three-year period beginning in 1928) to expand the research activities of the ICMA and to permit relocation of its national headquarters near the University of Chicago campus. Clarence E. Ridley, another friend of Brownlow's, was hired as the ICMA's new executive secretary to oversee the Chicago ICMA operations.

Ridley possessed the ideal qualifications for the position. He had been a city manager (of Bluefield, Virginia from 1921 to 1925) and vice-president of the ICMA, as well as a member of the academic community (Ph.D. from the Maxwell School, Syracuse University, and research associate at the National Institute of Public Administration in New York City).

Two years later, in 1930, the Spelman Fund gave monies to set up a center for several organizations concerned with public administration, the Public Administration Clearing House (PACH), near the University of Chicago campus (1313 East 60th Street). With a grant of $1,163,000, a permanent headquarters of PACH was built to house nine organizations in addition to the ICMA: the national headquarters of the Civil Service Assembly (now the Public Personnel Association), the Municipal Finance Officers Association, the American Legislators Association (now the Council of State Governments), the American Municipal Association (now the National League of Cities), the American Public Welfare Association, the American Society of Planning Officials, the American Public Works Association, the Public Administration Service, and the Governmental Research Association.

The new organization, PACH, was incorporated in December 1930 with Louis Brownlow, Richard Childs, and Luther Gulick designated as incorporators. The first director was Louis Brownlow, who served until 1945, when he was succeeded by Herbert Emmerich, who had been PACH's associate director since 1937.

The Spelman Fund support for the operations of the ICMA rose between 1930 and 1935 from 18 percent to 66 percent of the ICMA's operating revenue. During this period the fund provided $69,000 specifically for the association's research activities.

The Work of Louis Brownlow

Since Louis Brownlow appeared frequently as a central figure in the development of the city management profession and, in general, the field of public administration, it is worthwhile to consider his influence on the historical development of the profession. As Richard Childs had played an important role in fostering the council-manager plan, perhaps no individual was more instrumental than Louis Brownlow in creating the city manager's professional identity. As ICMA president, he had campaigned for a professional focus to the organization's work. Through his friendships with Merriam, Ruml, and Ridley, he was the key figure in locating its national headquarters at Chicago and providing ample research funding for its staff. What background and personality propelled him into his role as creator of a professional identity?

Louis Brownlow was a product of the late-nineteenth-century rural Middle West. His family had migrated to Missouri from Tennessee after the Civil War, and he was raised in a small town by parents who both taught school from time to time. Brownlow himself had little formal education. Illness kept him out of school during much of his childhood and poverty prevented him from going to college. His informal education, however, was extensive. He was a voracious reader. Even in his childhood he absorbed all varieties of literature, and his reading was supplemented by the family's animated dinner table discussions of religion and politics. The parents were traditional southern Democrats living in a Republican section of Missouri, which intensified political debates. Moreover, Sunday mornings were apt to find Father Brownlow with the Disciples of Christ, Mother Brownlow with the Methodists, and Louis left to choose one of the three Protestant denominations in the community. The family's intense interest in the ethical issues of small-town politics and religion might very well help to explain his later sense of mission regarding his public service career. "I look upon my profession as city manager in exactly the same way that a minister of the gospel looks upon his mission, and believe . . . I am doing on earth the work of the Master," Brownlow told his fellow city managers at the 1922 ICMA Convention.[46]

Brownlow, however, did not choose the ministry as a career, nor did he first seek government work. For several years he was a newspaper reporter in Washington, D.C. His work gave him a facility with words; his ability to express his thoughts was markedly superior to that of most of the early city managers, whose engineering training must have sharply limited their verbal skills. More important, journalism offered Brownlow a wide variety of human experiences and contacts associated with observing government firsthand. In this respect the whole panorama of life was his classroom, and his mind was not burdened with the traditional academic theories of government. In a remarkable book, a best seller in its day, *The American Government* (published under the name of Frederic Haskin but in fact written by Louis Brownlow),[47] Brownlow showed his early interest in and unique understanding of American government. Whereas other writers of that period had focused on the Congress or the presidency, Brownlow's book devoted twenty-four of its thirty-one chapters to the administrative structure of the government. His book presented a detailed and very accurate account of the workings of the separate departments of the executive branch.

Brownlow's freedom from doctrinal commitments also gave him a rare mobility among men. As his later life proved, he could move with astonishing ease among foundation people, academicians, civil servants, and U.S. presidents. His friendship, for example, with President Woodrow Wilson eventually secured him an appointment to the District Commissioners of Washington, D.C. where he served as one of three presidential appointees between 1915 and 1920.

Brownlow evidently enjoyed his experience in municipal administration as a Washington commissioner, for when his term expired in 1920, he moved to a city managership in nearby Petersburg, Virginia and later to Knoxville, Tennessee. In both manager jobs he served with an intense dedication, building new medical and health facilities where there had been none before, establishing public libraries where libraries had previously been private or nonexistent, and expanding all kinds of public services, from parks to playgrounds. The conscientious effort he put into his work, as well as his fights with the Ku Klux Klan and other political factions in Tennessee, eventually broke his health, and he was forced to resign his Knoxville managership. Nevertheless, his work earned him national recognition as well as the presidency of the ICMA.

As president of the ICMA, he applied the same sense of "mission" that he had shown in his building projects in local communities like Petersburg and Knoxville. He helped to establish ICMA national headquarters first in Kansas and then in Chicago, and he helped the ICMA to form a strong executive staff and a scholarly journal and gain foundation support for its expansion and university backing for its research. Most important, he pressed for a professional identity for the organization that would lend it stature and prestige. "I believe that the Association should leave to others the business of political propaganda . . . ," he wrote to his fellow managers in a 1923 editorial in the *City Manager Magazine*. But his plea for a professional identity was not based merely on selfish interest. Professionalism was very much connected in Brownlow's mind with a moral impulse to improve the general condition of mankind. We should assume, he told his fellow managers in the same editorial, "as we enter upon our tenth year that our profession is an established profession, that our association is a professional society and that our chief interest is in the work we are doing for mankind."[48]

As noted above, in many respects Brownlow was to the city manager profession what Richard Childs had been to the city manager movement—father, inventor, creator, and manipulator of symbols. Both were products of the Progressive age. Both had created ideologies—Childs, the manager plan, and Brownlow, manager professionalism—and both were successful in gaining institutional and academic support for their programs. Most of all, both men saw their individual efforts as a means of improving democracy and the quality of life for mankind. But whereas Childs was a doctrinaire liberal who sought basic reform of the American municipal structure, Brownlow pursued his reform ideals by means of "professionalizing" administration. Reform to him did not imply institutional change as much as improved institutional operation. Training, research, planning, accounting methods, merit principles, budgets were several of the professional tools he utilized for community improvement. If Childs had urged a fundamental reform of the municipal institutional structure in order to revitalize local democracy, Brownlow, the more pragmatic, nondoctrinaire, conservative, sought to make the *status quo* work more effectively. Both were Progressives, but they exhibited different tendencies. A Republican businessman, Childs was in many respects the institutional reformer, while Brownlow, as a Wilsonian Democrat, was much more deeply committed to the existing institutional structure. Their careers ended typically differently. Childs remained the darling of the municipal reform movement, still very much an outsider to the corridors of political power. Brownlow eventually went back to Washington as a key adviser to President Franklin Roosevelt, supervising government reorganization, and was always close to the "dilemmas of governance." Strange as it seems, the two old Progressives were as different as Tory and Whig, as Burke and Rousseau. And yet both in their respective ways were instrumental in creating the modern city manager profession.[49]

ICMA Research and the Flowering of Orthodox Taylorism

Through the leadership of Louis Brownlow, the academic support of Charles Merriam at the University of Chicago, and the financial contribution of the Spelman and Rosenwald funds, ICMA research flourished at Chicago during the late 1920s and the 1930s. The direction that these research activities took during this period had been largely established by an ICMA Committee on Research, chaired by Louis Brownlow, in 1928.[50] The several committee recommendations included undertaking studies of "governmental reporting," "municipal finance," "policy administration," and "city management."

Whereas books on the city manager during the 1910s and early 1920s had frequently amounted to reform tracts sponsored by the National Municipal League and other good government groups,[51] by the late 1920s and 1930s books appearing on city management had a different tone and emphasis, namely, that of scientific management. First, the ICMA began publishing reference sources on municipal activities which provided basic current facts and information on the operations of city government. Some of these were *Recent Trends in American Municipal Government* (1930), *What the Depression Has Done to Cities* (1935), *Social Characteristics of Cities* (1937); in 1934 the ICMA began publishing *The Municipal Year Book* as an annual data source on American cities.

During this era the ICMA also started to publish training books on the techniques of city management. Eight in-service training courses, established by the ICMA on a permanent basis, emphasized up-to-date techniques of efficient municipal administration in a number of specific fields. The basic texts were the voluminous "green book" series: *The Technique of Municipal Administration, Municipal Personnel Administration, Municipal Finance Administration, Municipal Police Administration, Local Planning Administration, Municipal Public Works Administration, Municipal Fire Administration,* and *Municipal Recreation Administration.*

Among broader writings on the city manager profession, it is worth examining two texts in particular as classic scientific management images of the city manager: Leonard White's *The City Manager* (1927) and Clarence E. Ridley and Orin F. Nolting's *The City Manager Profession* (1934).

Leonard White's *The City Manager* (1927) was the first book-length study of the city management profession, and in many ways it was a groundbreaking treatise in political science. White went to the University of Chicago in 1920 to study under Charles Merriam. Merriam, an early advocate of appointed executive government and the city manager plan, undoubtedly influenced White's initial choice of this subject for study, and, through the Social Science Research Council and the University of Chicago, he helped to secure financial support for White's research. Moreover, Merriam himself had previously examined the problems of democratic leadership by analyzing the lives, personalities, and activities of several political leaders.[52] White's methodology similarly focused on the manager's personality and activities. The first seven of the fourteen chapters of White's *The City Manager* are devoted to brief character sketches of leading managers of the era. During 1926 White traveled to over thirty American cities interviewing managers. The image of the men he interviewed was the very opposite of the nineteenth-century political party boss. According to White, they were men who *did* things instead of just talking about them. They were direct, honest, straightforward, and interested in management technique rather than political manipulation. "Managers have demonstrated a unique readiness to accept responsibility. . . . They do not 'pass the buck' but are forthright and straight forward. . . . They have been wholly unwilling to deceive the voters. . . . They have sought the support of the large interests of the city. . . ."[53]

In White's concluding chapter, he shows his deep admiration for managers as a new professional group as well as his own commitment to the concepts of scientific management. The gravest threats he saw to city managers were, first, "the failure of the city council" to allow "the manager to manage" by infusing politics into the area of administration; second, the manager's own ambitious "venturing" into matters of "policy"; third, the tendency of many councils to prefer "local men," thus making the manager's job an issue of partisan politics.

Clarence E. Ridley and Orin F. Nolting, respectively the director and assistant executive director of the ICMA, wrote *The City Manager Profession*, which appeared in 1934. Like White's book, this study was published at the University of Chicago with the sponsorship of the Rosenwald and Spelman funds channeled through the Public Administration Clearing House. It was dedicated to "those city managers who are striving to raise the art and science of public administration"; in its foreword Louis Brownlow wrote that city managers "represented a radical change in American notions of local government in the replacement of the amateur by the technician. . . ."[54]

White had attempted to study the manager realistically, through field interviews; only at the end did he clearly state his perspective of Taylorism. In contrast, Ridley and Nolting's book from the outset presented a concise summary of the orthodox scientific management ideology as it applied to city managers. Essentially the book offered a normative statement—rather than an empirical portrait—of the ideal position, qualifications, training, selection process, and professional attributes of the city manager. One chapter did contain a good statistical survey of managers in 1934, but the other seven constituted a series of statements of the scientific management philosophy.

Ridley and Nolting envisioned the manager's job as policy implementation; the council was seen as responsible for policy determination. "A small council elected at-large on a non-partisan ballot determines all municipal policies," and "the city manager is its agent charged with carrying out the policies."[55] The manager's qualifications were equated with the positive professional attributes of "decisiveness, drive, persistence, aggressiveness, forcefulness." Councils were warned to choose only "the properly trained and qualified people" and to make appointments on the basis of "ability and experience rather than on political affiliation and residence." The last chapter linked manager professionalism with the virtues of the "highest individual responsibility," "a desire for service," "a devotion to the highest standards of workmanship," and "professional knowledge." Nolting and Ridley succinctly combined the virtues of orthodox Taylorism with manager professionalism.

The Apex of the Generic Science of Municipal Administration: The 1938 ICMA Code

The acme of the influence of Taylorism on the city management profession was the adoption of the revised 1938 Code of Ethics at the ICMA Convention in Boston, Massachusetts (refer to Appendix D for full text).[56] It represented the most articulate application of the scientific management philosophy to the city manager's professional role. If the original 1924 code reflected the emergence of the managers' professional identity, the 1938 code showed the profession's commitment to the doctrines of Taylorism. In the revised 1938 code the words "administration" and "administrator" appeared prominently throughout the text, whereas in the 1924 code ethical qualities like "loyalty" and "responsibility" had been stressed. The city manager "is the administrator for all the people and handles each administrative problem without discrimination," the revised code declared. As a "professional administrator," he "resists any encroachment on his control," handling all matters "on the basis of merit." "The city manager is governed by the highest ideals of honor and integrity in all his public and personal relations in order that he may merit the respect and inspire the confidence of the administrative organization. . . ." "The city manager is in no sense a political leader"; rather he is first and foremost "a professional administrator."

Interestingly, the 1938 code deleted Section 7 of the 1924 code, which had recognized the manager's limited involvement in community politics: "Power justifies responsibility, and responsibility demands power, and a city manager who becomes impotent to inspire support should resign." Much sharper boundaries between politics and administration were drawn in the revised 1938 code. The 1924 code had left the door open to managers for policy involvement, but the 1938 revised code established the political-administrative dichotomy clearly.

The 1938 Code equated the competent city manager, free from political influence, with the highest form of good, and it saw city problems fundamentally as issues for effective management and administration. Planning, research, budgets were the tools of the manager for solving communities' dilemmas. Policy decisions were made by the council, but the manner of policy implementation had to be left up to the expertise of the manager.

This philosophy was the philosophy of the leaders of the city management profession—Brownlow, Ridley, and Nolting—and had been developed by their research at Chicago over the last decade. Also, scientific management had been the accepted doctrine during this period of such leaders of the academic world as Charles Merriam and Leonard White. And ample research funding through the Spelman and Rosenwald funds was available for its support.

The 1938 code marked the watershed of orthodox scientific management thinking on the city manager profession: the internal leadership of the ICMA accepted it, and the academic and foundation worlds supported it. Most leaders were certain that good administration was the highest form of city management and that bad administration was the worst possible evil.

Summary

If the Progressive reformer Richard Childs had fathered the liberal, doctrinaire, and popular ideals of the council-manager plan, Louis Brownlow, the guiding spirit of city manager professionalism, symbolized the more conservative side of the Progressive mind: pragmatic, rational, professionally oriented, and committed to strengthening local government through the tools of administration.

Brownlow's astute leadership welded together a unique triangle of supporters for manager professionalism: reformers, academicians, and foundations. Reformers created and sustained the growth of the plan, academicians gave it intellectual and popular appeal, and foundations provided monies for ICMA research and staff.

The ICMA's early commitment to a professional identity was symbolized by its 1924 Code of Ethics. The 1938 revised code represented the influence of a decade of scientific management research at its Chicago headquarters.

Much like Karl von Clausewitz's *Vom Kriege*, which provided an intellectual rationale for nineteenth-century military professionalism in Europe, scientific management, or Taylorism, furnished the twentieth-century city manager profession with its intellectual and theoretical bases. In its most fundamental formulation, Taylorism viewed good administration as the highest virtue and bad administration as the worst possible evil. The 1938 Code of Ethics clearly emphasized this doctrine. Yet ironically, the ink was hardly dry on the revised code when intellectual commitment to scientific management began to wane.

3

The Trials of the ICMA:
Ideological Confusion and Organizational Atrophy in the Postwar Era

Each profession makes progress, but it is progress in its own groove. Now to be mentally in a groove is to live in contemplating a given set of abstractions. The groove prevents straying across country and the abstraction abstracts from something to which no further attention is paid. But there is no groove of abstractions which is adequate for comprehension of human life.

Alfred North Whitehead
Science and the Modern World (1925)

The uneasiness that has now come to bother the manager profession traces in part to the fact that the lines that joined the ICMA circle to the circles marked universities, Brookings, and consultants in administration have become frayed, perhaps severed.

Gilbert Y. Steiner
*Long-Range Program for Urban
Management Research:
A Policy Statement* (1964)

Like an athlete the morning after his Olympic victory, the city manager appeared after World War II—at least to the older generation of political scientists—as something of a modern American hero. Writing in the pages of *Public Management* in 1945, the then-dean of the social science fraternity, Charles E. Merriam, concluded that "the greatest achievement of American administration is the city manager. He is a type par excellence in public administration, marked by integrity, by competence and by adjustability."[1] And in the same year before an august body of senior civil servants at the prestigious Graduate School of Public Administration, Harvard University, Clarence E. Ridley, executive director of the ICMA, propounded the basic verities of city management in an address, "The Job of the City Manager."[2]

But many Americans found such enthusiasm for managers and their attendant values of economy and efficiency foreign to the central issues facing the country in the postwar decades. The 1930s had shaken American confidence in the older virtues of rugged individualism, laissez-faire, and business ideals. The very real hardships of a long-term economic depression had caused a general public acceptance of the need for government intervention in the private sector. The decade had seen the welfare state replace the laissez-faire approach to solving societal problems.

Moreover, Hiroshima and Nagasaki had opened a new chapter in world history. Suddenly America was thrust into a role of international leadership and global responsibility. No longer could the United States maintain its traditional isolationist stance in foreign relations. It had become a permanent part of the international community and the single most influential country in the world. Finally, issues like racism came suddenly into national prominence. The racist policies of Adolf Hitler provoked a profound feeling of dissatisfaction with America's treatment of its own minorities. It seemed illogical to many citizens of this country to fight a world war in the name of the Four Freedoms and yet not to extend those same freedoms to its own citizens.

Caught in this whirlwind of new national experiences, the significance of scientific management, with its attendant values of economy and efficiency, suddenly paled in comparison to the pressing issues of the welfare state, foreign affairs, the atom bomb, and racism.

Administrators who were among the first to confront the dilemmas presented by these new issues began to question the older mechanistic formulas and values of Taylorism. Viewing the administration of the budget as part of wider political processes, Paul H. Appleby, a former assistant secretary of agriculture and assistant director of the Bureau of the Budget (later dean of the Maxwell School), wrote in 1948, "The budget is made not merely by technical processes, it is made in the field where mighty forces contend over it."[3] Most of Appleby's extensive writings hammered at this single theme: administration is not an isolated endeavor but is caught up in the complex web of national politics and moral values.

Younger postwar scholars also challenged the intellectual validity of many of the "truths" of scientific management. From the perspective of logical positivism, Herbert Simon's *Administrative Behavior* (1945) pointed out the numerous contradictions in "the principles of administration." "For almost every principle," wrote Simon, "one can find an equally plausible and acceptable contradictory principle."[4]

Dwight Waldo looked at American public administration through the long-range telescope of classical political theory and history in *The Administrative State* (1948). He saw public administration as rooted in the peculiar material and ideological climate of the American civilization. Waldo concluded that public administration thinking wrestled with the same eternal philosophic questions as the classic political theories: What is the purpose of government? What are the criteria for political action? Who should rule? Should political organization be centralized or decentralized? Should political power be unified or divided?[5]

The Professional Identity Crisis

To the postwar generation of American social scientists, who faced new national issues and had broader intellectual backgrounds than their predecessors had had, scientific management seemed not so much like a cultural hero as like Holden Caulfield, the youthful protagonist of *The Catcher in the Rye*—intellectually confused and personally in a state of identity crisis. For the city management profession that had so heartily embraced the doctrines of Taylorism prior to World War II, this new intellectual mood meant that the profession's central principles, values, and ideals suddenly became less relevant—even irrelevant—in coping with many of the new political and social issues the nation now faced.

In this era the city managers seemed to find themselves in a professional identity crisis; their role was uncertain in a modern world that was less than enthusiastic about the problems of municipal efficiency. "Who am I in modern American society?" was the central question managers grappled with repeatedly at their conferences and conventions and in their journal over the next twenty years. During this period numerous points of view about the profession's role competed for acceptance as *the* professional *Weltanschauung*.

Neo-Taylorism

It was perhaps symbolic that during September 1945, the very month World War II ended, Clarence Ridley's speech at Harvard University on "The Job of the City Manager" should have been reprinted in *Public Management*.[6] In essence, this speech attempted to define the role of the city manager in the modern postwar world. Eleven years before, in *The City Manager Profession*, Ridley, with Orin Nolting, had portrayed the city manager as a classic scientific manager—the almost mechanistic chief administrator of the municipality, who simply carried out the policies of the city council. Indeed, Ridley's 1945 speech reflected much the same view: "The job of the chief administrative officer of any public or private enterprise was to see that things get done." By this time, however, Ridley no longer conceived the manager's role quite so simply. More individual art and skill were required for a manager "to take a group of human beings and to mold them into a smooth functioning administrative organization." For Ridley, administrative results were still the prime objectives of the city manager's work, but achieving results was no longer merely a mechanical chore of translating a council's policies into administrative action. Considerable art and skill were now required on the part of individual practitioners.

Such "neo-Tayloristic" thinking was strongly apparent in several of the presidential addresses delivered at the annual ICMA conventions during the 1950s. John H. Ames, city manager of Ames, Iowa, for example, echoed this philosophy in his inaugural ICMA presidential address (1950) on "The Art of Management."[7] Like Ridley, Ames equated the city manager's role with producing results for the city he served. Nevertheless, results could only be achieved, according to Ames, by adequate "administrative experience" and by "understanding people." Ames believed that the job of city manager demanded few "technical qualifications" but ample "artistry of handling people in organizations."

The Policy Leadership and Human Relations School

Just prior to World War II an important book challenged the absolutism of the scientific management doctrines as they applied to city management. Harold A. Stone, Don K. Price, and Kathryn H. Stone's *City Manager Government in the United States* (1940) was a product of the Chicago school, published by the Committee on Public Administration of the Social Science Research Council, whose membership included Louis Brownlow and Leonard White. The book grew out of a 1937 nationwide study of "the results and practical operation of the city manager plan after its first 25 years of operation." The research, which was one of the earliest large-scale social science team efforts, was guided by Mr. and Mrs. Stone and Mr. Price and involved forty-eight professors and graduate students who systematically examined thirty-two manager communities around the United States. The Stone-Price-Stone volume summarized the results of thirty-two community case studies.[8]

Unlike Leonard White's *The City Manager* (1927), which had examined the character and qualities of individual managers, or the Ridley-Nolting 1934 investigation of the *City Manager Profession*, the Stone-Price-Stone book carefully surveyed the practice and operation of city manager government. It concluded that there was no absolute way to judge the performance of the city manager plan. The authors found that in many cities the plan had brought about several conspicuous changes: "a diminution of partisan or factional influence," "a more scientific or businesslike attitude in government," "further long-range planning," "more public spirited political leadership," and "increased prestige of municipal government." Yet the researchers believed that it was impossible to gauge precisely the results of manager government in any city. The manager plan in several cases may have reduced the unit cost of municipal services, but at the same time the quantity and quality of such services were often increased, thus raising the total cost to the taxpayer.

And to the surprise of the researchers, the city manager was hardly an inconspicuous administrator who merely followed the policy dictates of the city council. In practice they discovered no sharp differentiation between the idealized policy determination role of the city council and the policy implementation role of the manager. It is "generally impossible," the authors said, "for the city manager to escape being a leader in matters of policy, for it is an essential part of his administrative job to make recommendations." In summary, the researchers wrote, "These men have made great contributions in the technique of administration but they have made even greater contributions as leaders of municipal policy.[9]

The leadership theme of the Stone-Price-Stone study was popularized within the city management fraternity at the thirty-fourth annual ICMA conference, September 1948, at Mackinac Island, Michigan. In his inaugural presidential address, Manager C. A. Harrell of Norfolk, Virginia sought to answer the question: "To what extent should the city manager assume the status of a leader in his community? His answer was unequivocal:

> The ideal city manager is a positive, vital force in the community. He spends a great deal of his time thinking of the broad objectives which would greatly improve community life. Why should he hesitate to initiate policy proposals and submit them to council? Neither the mayor nor individual councilmen can give much time to this task and if the manager also shies away from such leadership, the community stands still and important matters are allowed to pass by default.

And Harrell concluded:

> Thus the city manager has a moral obligation to devise careful plans, policies if you will, for submission to the council. He is more than a mere administrator, he is a formulator of action and a planner. He does not limit himself to worship of gods of technique, procedures, and implementation. Rather he visualizes broad objectives, distant goals, farsighted projects.[10]

In another major address, at the 1948 ICMA conference, Herman G. Pope, director of the Public Administration Service in Chicago, echoed Harrell's leadership theme but addressed himself to the subject of "The City Manager as Leader in the Administration Organization." For Pope, the city manager exercised leadership principally within the confines of the city administration rather than the community at large: "The city manager as a leader must provide an opportunity for participation by subordinates in deciding how things are to be done." Pope saw the manager's "leadership role" in terms of "utilizing fully personnel capacities and other resources of the specialized staff."[11]

Both Harrell's and Pope's speeches generated considerable debate at the following ICMA conventions and in the pages of *Public Management.* These discussions may have reflected the managers' own uncertainty about their proper postwar role in American communities. To the surprise of longtime manager-watcher Don K. Price, "The whole discussions showed [that] city managers . . . seemed to be asking themselves questions about the techniques of relationships with people, in much the same spirit as they once asked questions about the techniques of paving or accounting."[12] At the manager conferences in the late 1940s and early 1950s a marked emphasis on the human-relations aspects of the job was exemplified by such panel discussion topics as "Training Employees in Public Relations," "Methods of Ascertaining What the Public Thinks of Municipal Policies, Activities, and Employees," and "How to Sell the City to the People."

The Organic View

Not all the leaders of the ICMA immediately embraced the new doctrines of policy leadership and human relations. One tardy convert was Clarence E. Ridley, the executive director of the ICMA. In 1934 Ridley, along with Orin Nolting in *The City Manager Profession,* had propounded the doctrine of scientific management as the basic philosophy of the profession. We have seen that by 1945 Ridley had shifted to a position of neo-Taylorism. After his retirement as executive director of the ICMA in 1958, he produced another policy statement reflecting another change in his position on the role of the city manager.

In a curious and rather complex document entitled *The Role of the City Manager in Policy Formulation,* Ridley once again wrestled with the question of the manager's role.[13] After a survey of eighty-eight city managers (funded by the Social Science Research Council), Ridley found that the city manager is indeed part of the policy-making process; "the city manager by the very nature of his job acts as a policy formulator." At the same time, however, the manager is not the sole originator of public policies. "Policy springs from many sources varying from casual telephone complaints to big civic projects backed by large and influential segments of the community. These sources plus those originating from the manager and department personnel account for 75 to 90 percent of all policies adopted by the city council."

"Managers," according to Ridley, "are well aware that policy determination is more than a roll call. More often it is a slow, deliberate process involving a considerable period of time and a whole series of actions taken on the part of many people." In the final analysis, however, Ridley found that "it is the duty of the city council to make the decisions on policy." "Managers indicate no desire whatever to be designated as leaders of their communities or any interest in challenging the power of the council, the directly elected representatives of the people. On the other hand, managers indicate willingness to accept the responsibility entailed in actively helping the council formulate policies with but one objective —that of making cities more livable."

In his last major writing on the city manager's role, then, Ridley seemed to accept the argument of the leadership school that the city manager was involved in the policy-making process but was very much both more and less than a leader, at least in the conventional sense of the term. Legally, policy determination was still the prerogative of the elected council. Council roll calls were important, though in reality policies grew from many sources and the city manager, by virtue of his central role in local administration, was a major policy source. Ultimately, the degree of an individual manager's leadership very much depended on the situation at hand—the type of community, the quality of the council, and the temperament of the manager. Between 1934 and 1958 Clarence E. Ridley had moved from the doctrinaire position of Taylorism to a much more elastic view of city management perhaps best termed the *organic* view.

The New Political Realism

Postwar political scientists, influenced by a variety of new methodological tools—case studies, systems analysis, role analysis, communications theory—began to study political processes and events with more analytical rigor, using more factual detail. Principally through the case study, which attempted to portray a slice of political reality by careful description of a single political event, social scientists began to view the city manager as an important actor in the urban political processes. The Inter-University Case Program published two important cases on city managers, demonstrating their significant policy involvement: *The Cambridge City Manager* by Frank C. Abbot (1952) and *A City Manager Tries to Fire his Police Chief* by Frank P. Sherwood (1963). Also, in the early 1960s, the Harvard-MIT Joint Center for Urban Studies issued two community case studies that pointed up the city manager's enormous influence in community decision making: *A Report on Politics in Greater Miami* by Edward Sofen (1961) and *A Report on Politics in San Diego* by David Greenstone (1962). A spate of books, frequently funded by large social science research grants,[14] appeared in the 1960s, utilizing similar case study techniques and arriving at similar conclusions—namely, that the city manager acted in a political context.[15]

Perhaps the normative beliefs of the new political realism school in regard to city managers were best summarized in an article by Karl Bosworth.[16] Bosworth contended that the city manager was "a local politician" and that he significantly affected the distribution of community power, principally through his central control of municipal administration, his policy recommendations to the city council, and his control over the preparation of the city budget.

However, the conclusions of Bosworth and other "realistic" political scientists seemed to have had little influence on the city management profession.[17] It was not that the managers were unaware of these studies; rather, what the "realists" discovered seemed somehow unrealistic or irrelevant to the professional concerns of the city managers. Most experienced managers were sophisticated enough to realize that their work was indeed involved in community political processes, and at almost every manager conference since the ICMA was formed in 1914, discussions had been held on the political problems of council-manager relations. Particularly since Manager Harrell's 1948 presidential address, community leadership had been a popular theme within the manager profession.

Compared to political scientists, furthermore, city managers were largely concerned with a different set of questions. The issues that faced them did not center on the question of whether or not they were involved in the political processes, but rather focused on what they should do—for their cities' survival and their own survival—given the political situation. In some cities, this sort of survival depended on the development of policies designed to cope with issues of race, public housing, or the police; in other communities it meant finding solutions to the more routine line functions of government: waste removal, fire protection, and building codes. In these pressing areas the political "realists" had few answers, and thus their writings seemed, for the most part, removed from the immediate concerns of local government, at least from the managers' perspective. For managers, in short, the real problem was not "Who rules?" but "How to survive."

The Orthodox Reform Doctrines

If the writings of political "realists" seemed irrelevant to the daily problems of city administration, so too did the older reform doctrines of the National Municipal League. Throughout the post–World War II decades, Richard Childs and the members of the National Municipal League continued to advocate the orthodox reform doctrines as elaborated in their Model City Charter, little changed from the original 1915 version, which recommended the council-manager plan as the ideal form of municipal government. In 1963 Richard Childs, the eternal American reformer, was still vigorously propounding his views on the proper role of the manager. "The city manager," Childs emphasized, "should always keep in mind he is subordinate to a council's decision. He should never promote or defend a council's decision until it has been publicly adopted by council. . . ."[18] Somehow these dogmatic assertions by the old reformer seemed removed from the real world of city management in the turbulent postwar era, at least from the practitioner's perspective.

The 1952 Code of Ethics: The Search for an Ideological Consensus

With the proliferation of views on city management—neo-Taylorism, policy leadership and human relations, organicism, new political realism, and orthodox reform doctrines—the leadership of the ICMA felt a need to incorporate the new thinking into the ICMA Code of Ethics. The 1938 code had reflected a decade of scientific management research at Chicago and had stressed Taylorism as the central professional ideology. By the 1950s this philosophy seemed simplistic, mechanical, and out of date, and at the 1952 ICMA Convention the code of ethics was again revised.

In comparison to the 1938 code, the revised 1952 version seeks a basis for accommodation with the new philosophies. The 1938 code emphasizes that "the city manager is in no sense a political leader." In the 1952 code the reverse assumption is almost axiomatically accepted: "The city manager as a community leader submits policy proposals to the council and provides the council with facts and advice on matters of policy. . . ." Deleted in the new code was the section that had stressed that the city manager should keep "himself in the background by emphasizing the importance of facts." Also deleted were several colorless references to the city manager as "an administrator"; he was now conceived as having "a constructive, creative, and practical attitude toward urban problems."

The 1952 code broadened the policy responsibilities of managers, but this change was somewhat deceptive because, like the 1938 code, the 1952 code still linked the city management profession to the city manager plan: "No member of the profession accepts a position as city manager unless he is fully in accord with the principles of council-manager government." This meant that all the older reform doctrines of Taylorism could slide into the 1952 code through the back door, so to speak. Managers had to pay the appropriate respects to the scientific management doctrines in the council-manager plan while being policy leaders in their respective communities.

Organizational Atrophy in the Postwar Decades

If the 1930s had been a period of vitality and growth for the ICMA, the postwar decades represented an era of stagnation. Paradoxically, from the standpoint of finances and other statistical indicators, the ICMA was a thriving organization. Between 1945 and 1963, revenues exceeded income every fiscal year, and total revenue increased sevenfold in twenty-one years ($69,200 in 1945 to $511,300 in 1966).[19] The membership grew from 827 in 1945 to 4000 in 1967, and the full-time ICMA staff tripled in size. During the same period, the total number of manager cities nearly quadrupled.

But despite the outward appearance of affluence and success, the ICMA suffered serious organizational difficulties. To begin with, the management profession had had three sources of external support before World War II: foundations, reformers, and academicians. In the postwar era, support from these three groups sharply declined and often, in fact, was nonexistent.

In 1947 the Spelman Fund support for the ICMA ended and in 1949 the Spelman Fund ceased to exist altogether. Large foundation support in the social sciences shifted to radically different interests, among them large-scale hard science research efforts, such as attitude survey and opinion sampling conducted at the University of Michigan, multivariate analysis and input-output analysis at Harvard University, information theory and cybernetics at the Massachusetts Institute of Technology, decision modeling at the Carnegie Institute of Technology, cost-benefit and PPBS (Planning-Programming-Budgeting System) research at the Rand Corporation, and conflict resolution and game theory at the University of Michigan.[20]

A second reason for the lack of support for the profession was that old municipal reformers like Richard Childs, who had fought long and hard for the council-manager plan, had now passed from prominence in the reform movement. The new postwar reform groups, like the Americans for Democratic Action (ADA), Students for a Democratic Society (SDS), and the Southern Non-Violent Coordinating Committee (SNCC), turned their attention to problems such as civil rights and peace campaigns and away from municipal reform.

Finally, the support for the management profession from the academic community suddenly evaporated in the 1950s. Charles Merriam in 1945 had extolled management as "the greatest achievement of public administration"; writing in 1964, Professor Gilbert Y. Steiner found that:

> the lines from ICMA to the Social Science Research Council no longer exist. Nor have fresh lines to new agencies of comparable quality been established. There is no certainty that a community of

interests exists between the city manager profession and the Regional Science Association or the American Management Association, or the Operations Research Society of America or the Rand Corporation, but it is clear that men of high intelligence are working in these groups, that their work commands attention in professional circles tangential to urban management, and that channels of communication between them and the city manager profession are not now adequate.[21]

The withdrawal of external support for the ICMA was attributable in part to four major internal difficulties of the ICMA during this era. First, the ICMA headquarters, which in 1928 had been situated at the hub of public administration and municipal government thinking near the University of Chicago campus, was now remote from the center of metropolitan policy making in the postwar period. The federal government had become the center of strategic decisions affecting urban growth and change after World War II. During the 1950s, and even more during the 1960s, the federal government became involved in an astonishing array of local activities: low rent public housing, urban renewal, civil defense, civil rights, job retraining, sewage treatment, hospital grants, harbor and river improvements, National Guard armories, air and water pollution controls, mental health, public health, school aid, libraries, airport and highway construction, FBI training for local law enforcement officials. ICMA headquarters at Chicago became increasingly isolated from the critical federal decisions affecting American cities.

Secondly, in addition to geographic isolation, the ICMA suffered from a leadership vacuum. Throughout the 1950s and early 1960s the executive directorship of the ICMA was held by Clarence E. Ridley (1928–56) and Orin F. Nolting (1956–66). Before becoming executive director, Nolting had been Ridley's assistant since 1928, and so each had thirty years or more of service to the ICMA. Both had served the organization well, but now were in their fifties and sixties, which caused a certain rigidity in their approach to the modern dilemmas of the ICMA and the city management field in general. Furthermore, both men had been deeply involved in the scientific management research conducted at the University of Chicago during the 1930s; Ridley had actually held a part-time appointment on the Chicago political science faculty. Their involvement with the development of Taylorism sharply restricted their creative vision and ability to adapt the ICMA to the new demands of the postwar decades. Clarence Ridley, the more intellectually flexible of the two men, did alter his views quite remarkably, as we have seen in comparing his early views in *The City Manager Profession* (1934) with his later ideas in *The Role of the City Manager in Policy Formulation* (1958). However, Ridley was never really able to move beyond the scientific management mentality. Handicapped by a pre–World War II administrative philosophy, the central leadership of the ICMA found it hard to understand and then to adjust to the new forces shaping metropolitan America.[22] Subsequently, the leadership of the ICMA became increasingly isolated at the Chicago headquarters from the newer types of university academicians, the centers of urban policy making in Washington, D.C., and the different reform elements in American society.

Furthermore, the leadership vacuum at the ICMA headquarters was exacerbated by the peculiar organizational structure of the ICMA. The formal structure gave the executive director unusual informal control over policy-making responsibilities. The ICMA president, normally a leading city manager, is elected each year at the annual national ICMA convention and is a full-time practitioner, which means that, compared to the executive director and his staff, the president has limited time to formulate ICMA policy. To make matters worse, the ICMA staff under Ridley and Nolting suffered from a high turnover rate (only three of the entire staff itself had served a full decade from 1956 to 1966), and generally the staff itself was rather young and inexperienced (the average age in 1966 was twenty-six). Low pay was one of the principal reasons for the high turnover and youthfulness of the executive staff. Nevertheless, the effect of the frequent changes of presidents and executive staff tended to centralize the informal policy activities in the executive director's office, which only lent more weight to the outdated and somewhat doctrinaire scientific management views of Ridley and Nolting. Paradoxically, then, the formally decentralized democratic structure of the ICMA, with its frequent elections for president, produced highly centralized informal control over the decision-making apparatus of the organization.[23]

Finally, perhaps the greatest weakness of the ICMA was its failure to discipline members in even the most flagrant cases of professional irresponsibility. Article 8 of the revised 1961 constitution (Sections 1 and 2) provided that: "The executive board shall establish a standing Committee on Professional Conduct and adopt rules of procedure for its operation. . . . The executive board may censure, suspend or expel a member and shall notify him of its action. . . ."

In 1962 the activities of City Manager Mitchell of Newburgh, New York gained national attention through an investigation conducted by the New York State Welfare Commission regarding Mitchell's alleged actions in keeping eligible persons off the welfare rolls. These charges were later proved true. Moreover, the Executive Board of the ICMA discovered that Mitchell had made a speech on November 1, 1961, prior to the city council elections, before the Newburgh Women's Republican Club, in which he offered to resign if certain council members were not reelected and in which he challenged the mayor to resign if the candidates Mitchell supported were not elected to the council.[24] Despite Mitchell's open violation of professional ethics and clearly irresponsible use of his manager's position, the ICMA Executive Board, after carefully reviewing the case, chose only to censure his actions and not to strike his name from ICMA membership. If the work of the early city managers like Brownlow, Carr, Ashburner, Waite, and Edy represented the city management profession at its best, the Mitchell affair symbolized the profession in its worst and most impotent form.

The New Professionalism: The Revitalization of the ICMA in the Mid-1960s

During the mid-1960s, four important changes occurred to strengthen the manager profession: the ICMA moved its headquarters to Washington, D.C., expanded its research activities, appointed a new executive director, and revised its code of ethics.

In 1966 a comprehensive study was undertaken to determine the feasibility of moving the association headquarters to Washington, D.C. The report concluded that the ICMA should end its long association with the University of Chicago and the cluster of public administration organizations housed near the campus and develop closer ties with the federal government's growing influence in metropolitan affairs. In 1967 the ICMA established its new headquarters in Washington at 1140 Connecticut Avenue, only a short distance from the major federal centers of metropolitan policy making—the departments of Housing and Urban Development; Health, Education, and Welfare; and Transportation.

Secondly, at the ICMA Headquarters a vigorous research program, chaired by Gilbert Y. Steiner, professor of political science at the University of Illinois, was undertaken upon the recommendation of a well-written and convincing study, *Long-Range Program for Urban Management Research* (1964). Reminiscent of the 1928 Brownlow research committee report, Steiner's committee report enumerated several important areas where the ICMA could "contribute to the flow of information on urban management problems and contribute to professional growth."[25] Following the suggestions of the Steiner Report, several new books and monographs on city management began appearing, written by professors and professionals in the field and focusing on important areas of topical interest to practicing managers.[26]

Thirdly, in 1967 the ICMA selected Mark Keane as a successor to Orin Nolting. Keane's appointment to the executive directorship marked an important change in the leadership of the ICMA.[27] Whereas Ridley and Nolting had been associated with pre–World War II city management, Keane was a product of the postwar era. He had served as city manager of several communities, including Tucson, Arizona, had been an ICMA vice-president, and in 1964 had become president of the association. He had also held a position as director of land and facilities administration with the U.S. Department of Housing and Urban Development (HUD). His postwar city management work, combined with his high-level federal civil service experience, ideally suited the new image and needs of the ICMA. Keane's appointment symbolized the shift away from the influence of the Chicago school, with its attendant scientific management values, and toward a more pragmatic federal orientation.

Finally, the ICMA revised its code of ethics in 1969. Like the revisions of 1924, 1938, and 1952, the 1969 code revision marked a new chapter in the history of the city management profession. The 1924 code had introduced professionalism as the manager's occupational ideal; the 1938 code had reflected the spirit of scientific management research conducted during the 1930s at the Chicago school, and the 1952 code revision had attempted to find an ideological consensus among the competing old and new professional philosophies. Now, seventeen years later, another revision evidenced a new shift in the city management doctrines—perhaps a more radical change than any previous revision.

The first paragraph of the 1952 code had read, "No member of the profession accepts a position as city manager unless he is fully in accord with the principles of council-manager government." The 1969 revision dropped any reference to allegiance to the council-manager plan; instead the code simply required a member's dedication "to the concepts of effective and democratic local government." The city management profession, long wed to the reform ideals of the council-manager plan, had now parted company with that plan. Modern city managers were considered public management professionals, no longer tied to any specific form of local government. ICMA membership was opened to any professional practitioner in urban administration: county managers, business administrators, chief administrative officers, as well as city managers. The 1969 code deleted any specific mention of city managers. The code itself was renamed—it was now "The City Management Code of Ethics"—and the ICMA changed its own name from the International City Managers' Association to the International City Management Association.

Summary

After its growth in the years before World War II, the city management profession in the two postwar decades suffered from organizational stagnation and decline. During the 1930s managers had embraced scientific management so ardently that the profession had difficulty adapting to the trends and ideas of contemporary America. Moreover, the strength of the three major groups of prewar supporters of the ICMA—reformers, foundations, and academicians—melted away in the modern era.

Finally, the ICMA was handicapped by four major internal problems: its geographic isolation at Chicago, its weak central leadership, its peculiar organizational structure, which tended to leave policy making to the executive director, and its inability to enforce its own professional standards of conduct.

The mid-1960s, however, showed a trend toward a new professionalism. The ICMA shifted its headquarters to Washington, D.C., revised its code of ethics, selected Mark Keane as executive director, and established an ambitious research agenda.

Perhaps the clearest indication of the shift toward a new professionalism was the difference between the three postwar ICMA executive directors. Clarence Ridley was an academician turned ICMA Director (1928–56) who became the creative spokesman for Taylorism within the city management fraternity. Orin Nolting, his successor (1956–66), was an in-house appointee and a man who operated very much according to routine at the ICMA in the twilight of the dying scientific management doctrines. Mark Keane, appointed in 1967, had prior work experience both as a city manager and federal bureaucrat, and his own operating style could be characterized as pragmatic, professional, and Washington oriented.

4

The Modern City Manager:
A 1971 Profile of a Public Professional
in American Local Government

The City of Sumter hereby announces that applications will be received from now till December the first for the office of City Manager of Sumter.

This is a rapidly growing manufacturing city of 10,000 population, and the applicant should be competent to oversee public works, such as paving, lighting, water supply, etc. An engineer of standing and ability would be preferred. State salary desired and previous experience in municipal work. . . .

> First Advertisement for a City Manager,
> Sumter, South Carolina,
> October 14, 1912

Jackson, N.J. (18,500)—Past salary $14,500. Municipal administration; 1 person holding position since 1970. Ordinance passed 2/16/70. Appointed by: 3-member committee. Degree in public administration, business administration or related field plus municipal administration or assistant experience. Send resume to John C. Kiebler, township clerk, Municipal Building, R.D. 4, Box 52, 08527.

> Recent Advertisement for a City Manager,
> Jackson, New Jersey,
> February 1, 1971

Who is the city manager of the 1970s? What is he like as a person? Does he have a characteristic career pattern and work habits? How do contemporary managers compare with early city managers? Does the modern city manager possess a unique individual identity that distinguishes him from the average American citizen as well as from the early pioneers of the city management profession?

The Modern Manager: A 1971 Profile

Personal Characteristics

The twenty-three hundred American city managers reflect several striking statistical similarities.[1] To begin with, managers are a masculine group. Less than 1 percent are women (a recent survey located only seven woman city managers, mostly in small eastern and southern communities).[2] Managers are also predominantly white, native born, and Protestant (few are black,[3] less than 1 percent are foreign born, and 84 percent are Protestant).[4] This is particularly astonishing in a nation that is 13 percent Negro and only 34 percent Protestant. While their ages range from twenty-five to seventy-five, city managers are by and large middle-aged men (nearly two-thirds are between thirty-one and fifty years old). Their average age is between forty-three and forty-four, which is old by comparison to the national average age, now between twenty-six and twenty-seven. Ninety-seven percent report being married; the national average is 69 percent for that age group.

Their political affiliations tend very much to reflect regional differences. Of southern city managers, 93 percent list a preference for the Democratic Party, while better than three-fourths of northern, midwestern, and far western city managers prefer the Republican. Twenty-six percent were born in the northeastern states (23 percent are presently working as managers in the Northeast), and almost three-fifths were born in the middle western and southern states. This last statistic reflects another regional bias, since approximately 40 percent of the American population presently lives in the Northeast.

Very few managers came from professional families (2 percent) or families where the father was engaged in some public service occupation (7 percent); more than two-thirds (68 percent) came from families in small business, the trades, or clerical work (which is not surprising since even today only 14 percent of employees are classified by the United States Census as "professional" or "technical").[5] As for their own backgrounds prior to entering city management, 64 percent of the city managers report having held business or engineering positions and 29 percent engaged in some form of public service occupation before taking a manager's post.

In general, city managers are well educated. Sixty-nine percent are college graduates or have had advanced graduate training. Another 26 percent report having at least some college training. This is abnormally high compared to the national average, which indicates that only 16 percent of the United States population has graduated from college. Whereas three-quarters of the country's population are high school graduates, 98 percent of city managers have graduated from high school.

Of the college graduates, nearly 40 percent were trained in the liberal arts and another one-third in engineering disciplines (older managers tend to have had more engineering training in college than have younger managers). Managers who have failed for one reason or another to complete college or who lack a background in public administration frequently make up for the deficiency by taking one of the many ICMA correspondence training programs.

City managers work primarily in small and middle-sized communities. Seventy-nine percent work in cities with populations under twenty-five thousand, and only 4 percent of professional managers are in cities with populations over one hundred thousand (though only 5 percent of American communities have populations greater than one hundred thousand and 73 percent are below twenty-five thousand).Wherever they live, managers are deeply involved in their communities. Ninety-one percent report living in the city where they work and belonging to an average of more than five clubs or organizations. Most frequently they belong to professional, business, service, or church groups. Often they are involved in veterans and fraternal organizations. Less often they belong to cultural, sports, hobby, or political groups. Not only are they joiners, but they also hold a significant number of leadership positions in these groups; an average manager holds between one and three such offices.[6]

By standards of income, city managers belong to the upper middle class. While salaries for managers range from below $5,000 to over $40,000, the average manager earns $18,000, which is considerably better than the national average family income of $8,632. By comparison, the managers' average salary approximates a salary of a GS-13 or GS-14 rating in the federal civil service—a middle executive career level. According to the U.S. Census (1970), city managers' incomes compare favorably with other professional salaries: physicans and dentists, $25,141; lawyers and judges, $22,734; airline pilots, $19,176; physicists, $15,545; mathematicians, $15,495; engineers, $13,984; accountants, $12,537; secondary school teachers, $9,789.

Career Pattern and Work Characteristics

Managers have begun their work in city management at various ages, ranging from twenty-three to seventy, but 71 percent took their first city managerships when they were between twenty-three and forty years of age, with a significant percentage of these beginning in their late twenties or early thirties. Only 29 percent took their first posts after they were forty-one. Forty-two percent have managed more than one community, and a few have served in as many as five or six communities. Their length of tenure now averages approximately five years, with tenures ranging from less than two months to over twenty-six years). Those that have served as manager in other communities average eight years prior managerial experience.

Few managers were born in the communities they serve (only 6 percent), but their local roots are, nevertheless, quite strong. Fifty-four percent were born in the state where they now serve, and of those that went to college or university, 62 percent did so in the state where they now reside. Interestingly, the managers fit the national norm: 54 percent of American citizens live in the state in which they were born.

Thirty-six percent indicated that they chose to work in city management during their college or graduate school educations, 31 percent cite a job after school as the point at which they made their occupational choice, and 33 percent list "other sources." Few (1 percent) specifically cite a parent as the source of encouragement for entering city management; 17 percent list "friends"; 26 percent, "teachers"; 31 percent, "employers"; and 25 percent, "others."

Twenty-six percent give their principal reason for first seeking a city manager's job as "a desire for public service," and 22 percent list "career development" as the main reason. One-fifth cite "a vocational interest," and the same percentage simply say that they were "offered the position." Over half (55 percent) believe that their administrative or executive experience was the major reason why they were selected for the position. Three other major reasons given for their selection (9 percent each) are: "experience in finance and budgeting," "local ties," and "the recommendation of the former city manager."

Seventy-six percent of the managers claim "public service" and a devotion to "building the community" to be their greatest source of satisfaction from their work. Very few find the financial rewards (4 percent) or public recognition (1 percent) the greatest benefits accruing from the job. On the negative side, three-quarters of all managers surveyed claim that the greatest sources of dissatisfaction in their work are "the constant demands," "no time left for family life," and "political pressures." Eighteen percent cite "job insecurity" and "public apathy" as principal problems.

If they left city management, 27 percent of the managers said they would enter other fields of public service or teaching, 40 percent preferred "a business career," 14 percent would simply retire, and an unusually large percentage (9 percent) specifically cited "consulting work" as a second career.

The job of the city manager in 97 percent of the cities surveyed is full-time work (in 3 percent it is part-time work, and in several cities it is combined with another municipal job such as city engineer). The average manager works fifty-three hours per week (nearly four-fifths claim to work between fifty and sixty hours per week) and spends two or three evenings a week out on official business. Managers' heaviest job responsibilities center on general municipal administration. Asked about the formal managerial responsibilities specified by charter or ordinance, 64 percent of the managers surveyed feel that the function that requires their greatest time and effort during the year is "supervising all or most parts of city government." Eighteen percent state that "preparing the annual budget and administering it after adoption" take the most time. Six percent specifically cite "advising and reporting to the city council" as their most time-consuming activity.

The size of the manager's immediate staff tends to vary with the size of the community. In towns with fewer than ten thousand people, managers very often have only one secretary in their offices; in the largest cities, managers may have as many as two dozen people on their immediate staffs.

Thoughts on the City Management Profession

When asked to compare their job to other occupations, only 2 percent of the managers surveyed believed that their work was "not a profession in any sense of the word." Twenty-three percent felt that city management was "an established profession like law or medicine." Nearly three-quarters, however, saw it as more akin to an established public profession such as diplomacy or a new public profession such as city planning.[7]

Most were optimistic about the future of city management. Fifty-one percent envisioned more suburbs and middle-sized cities adopting manager government; and 34 percent felt that although their posts may be called by names other than *city manager* (i.e., *chief administrative officer*), professional urban management will increasingly be accepted by American communities. Only 4 percent believed that the number of manager cities would stay roughly the same size, and only 3 percent saw the number of manager cities as declining in the future.

Asked what core skills were essential for effective modern city management, managers considered the four most important skills to be (in order of descending importance): the ability to manage public programs and to develop new ones; human relations and public relations skills; budgeting and finance expertise; personnel and labor relations skills. Few saw highly specialized skills such as computer skills or planning and renewal expertise as essential for the professional practitioner.

One of the oldest issues in the city management field is the degree to which managers should exercise leadership in their communities. Surprisingly, there was near unanimity on the idea that the city manager was in some way a community leader. Only 8 percent of those surveyed saw themselves simply as administrators carrying out the council's policies. Twenty-eight percent favored "frequent, aggressive community leadership," 16 percent felt "the city manager should confine his exercise of leadership to within the city administration," and 14 percent felt that "leadership should be confined to aiding the city council in determining policy issues."[8]

Interestingly, when compared to other professional values and ideals, community leadership was rarely considered the most important professional ideal: only 4 percent of the city managers saw it as such. Nearly half (49 percent) considered their most important professional ideal to be "handling all matters on the basis of merit, fairness, and impartiality." And evenly ranked at 14 percent each were three other ideals: "giving community service," "carrying out council's policies," and "placing the 'good' of the community above 'own personal good.'"

Asked about preparation for the profession, 39 percent of those surveyed thought that training in public administration was the best preparation for city management; 23 percent simply felt that on-the-job training was the most valuable; only 5 percent favored studying "university liberal arts"; 8 percent, law; 12 percent, engineering; 8 percent, business; and 8 percent, political science.

By far the most popular idea for improving the quality of the city management profession was an improved training program, chosen by fifty-six percent of those surveyed. From the previous question, however, we can see that managers prefer functional training in administrative work to more general liberal arts education. Among the other suggested programs for improving the profession, 11 percent of the managers favored "a stronger professional association"; 13 percent, "a career retirement program"; 10 percent, "contracts for managers"; 9 percent, "licensing city managers"; and a few wanted "a better code of ethics," "better salaries," and "an improved public relations program for the profession."

Only one-third of the city managers surveyed answered the last question, which asked them to "name the city manager you consider to be the *best* practitioner in the field (past or present manager)." Of those who did answer this question, most gave the name of a local man in a nearby city. Among the nationally recognized managers who were nominated, the name of L. P. (Perry) Cookingham, former manager of Kansas City, appeared three times more frequently than that of any other major nominee. Also Carleton Sharpe, former manager of Hartford and Kansas City; Bert Johnson, of Arlington, Virginia; Thomas Fletcher, of San Jose, California; and Mark Keane, present executive director of the ICMA, received a substantial number of votes.[9]

Past and Present City Managers:
A Statistical Comparison

Has the statistical profile of city managers as a group changed over the years? How do modern managers compare quantitatively with pre–World War II city managers? What are the differences and similarities between the two groups?

Probably the most detailed statistical study of city managers prior to World War II was undertaken in the early 1930s by Clarence E. Ridley and Orin F. Nolting and published in their book, *The City Manager Profession.*[10]

A comparison of their data with the results of the 1971 Maxwell Survey shows that modern city managers are somewhat younger than their predecessors were (see Table 1). A considerably higher number of

TABLE 1
The Age Distribution of City Managers

Ages	1971 Maxwell Survey	1934 Ridley-Nolting Survey
Under 30	26%	7%
31-40	45	34
41-50	21	37
51-60	5	19
Over 61	3	3

managers today are under thirty, indicating that managers are starting in the field at an earlier age. Whereas the mean age was found to be forty-seven to forty-eight years old in the Ridley-Nolting survey, the average manager's age in 1971 had dropped to between thirty-eight and thirty-nine. The fact that both studies found only 3 percent over sixty-one years old indicates that city management has always been a relatively young man's game.

The geographic concentration of city manager communities in the South and Midwest remains quite evident today (see Table 2). Slightly over half the nation's manager communities are located in these regions—a decline from 74 percent in 1934. The postwar growth of suburban and middle-sized manager communities in Southern California, Texas, and the Northeast largely accounts for the declining concentration of manager communities in the Midwest and South.

Most managers today, as in 1934, work in communities with populations of fewer than twenty-five thousand (see Table 3). Both then and now, approximately four-fifths of managers were in cities below that size. In both eras less than 10 percent of the managers worked in cities of over fifty

TABLE 2

The Geographic Distribution of Manager Cities[11]

Region	1971 Maxwell Survey	1934 Ridley-Nolting Survey
Northeast	23%	13%
Southeast	27	36
Midwest	27	38
Southwest	17	10
Northwest	6	3

thousand people and between one-quarter and one-third were in towns of fewer than five thousand. The striking fact, however, is the tremendous growth of manager communities for each population category. The percentage of manager cities for each category has either doubled or tripled between 1934 and 1971 to the point where today over half the cities of between twenty-five thousand and one hundred thousand have managers, compared to approximately one-quarter of those cities in 1934. This seems to indicate a trend toward manager government, particularly in middle-sized American cities over the last thirty-seven years. However, the percentage of manager cities still remains much lower among the very largest and very smallest American communities.

TABLE 3

Size of Manager Communities

Size (In Thousands)	1971 Maxwell Survey		1934 Ridley-Nolting Survey	
	% of Total Number of Manager Cities	% of Cities that are Manager Cities	% of Total Number of Manager Cities	% of Cities that are Manager Cities
Over 500	1	19	0	0
100-500	3	48	1	18
50-100	6	54	6	27
25-50	12	52	10	20
10-25	26	48	23	18
5-10	22	41	34	8
Under 5	30	12	26	N.A.

N.A. = Not Available

From the standpoint of educaton, city mangers today are considerably better educated and have broader educational backgrounds than pre–World War II managers. Tables 4 and 5 note a significant increase in the number of college-trained managers and in the number educated in the liberal arts, as well as a sharp decrease in the number of engineering majors.

TABLE 4

Highest Educational Attainment

Educational Level	1971 Maxwell Survey	1934 Ridley-Nolting Survey
Masters or Advanced Degrees	27%	13%
B.A. or B.S.	42	51
Some College	26	N.A.
High School	3	21
Grade School	2	15

TABLE 5

College Majors

(Those with B.A. or B.S. Degrees)

Majors	1971 Maxwell Survey	1934 Ridley-Nolting Survey
Liberal Arts	39%	6%
Engineering	33	77
Public Administration	12	3
Business Administration	14	N.A.
Agriculture	2	N.A.

A similar shift away from engineering backgrounds is also noticeable in the statistics on occupations managers have engaged in prior to entering city management (see Table 6). However, there is a marked increase in business backgrounds.

TABLE 6

Occupations Prior to Entering City Management

Occupations	1971 Maxwell Survey	1934 Ridley-Nolting Survey
Government Service	29%	42%
Business	47	28
Engineering	16	21
Other	8	9

Not only is the modern city manager better and more broadly trained, but he is increasingly less a "hometown boy." Between 1931 and 1933 (depression years) Ridley and Nolting classified about two-thirds of the managers as hometown appointments. Today only 6 percent of the managers were born in the communities they now serve; as previously pointed out, however, their local ties tend to be quite strong—54 percent were born in the state where they now serve, and 62 percent of those with college degrees went to the state university or college. The average tenure of city managers both in 1934 and 1971 remains slightly over five years.

Managers' salaries have more than doubled—often they have even tripled—over the last thirty-seven years, to the point where they compare favorably with federal civil service pay scales and are more than twice as high as the present average national family income (see Table 7).

TABLE 7

Average Manager Salaries by Population Grouping

City Size (In Thousands)	1971 (Comparable GS Rating Pay Scales—1971)	1934
Over 250	$33,000 (GS-17)	N.A.
100-250	25,769 (GS-16)	$12,134
50-100	23,000 (GS-15)	6,361
25-50	19,635 (GS-14)	5,865
10-25	15,900 (GS-12)	4,100
5-10	9,575 (GS-8)	3,091
Under 5	7,675 (GS-6)	2,329
Average Manager Salary for All Cities $18,000		5,100 (1930)
Average National Family Income $ 8,632		4,100 (1930)

Two Impressions from the Survey Data

The Three Worlds of the City Manager: Large City, Suburb, Small Town

One distinct impression gained from studying the 1971 Maxwell Survey data on city managers is that the size of the community tends to define the manager's activities; that is to say, in most cases, the population size of the community tends to determine the allocation of the manager's time.[12]

In the very largest cities, especially those with populations over one hundred thousand, managers are less involved with the daily routines of the actual line operations of their cities. Policy matters, planning activities, intergovernmental relations, reporting to council, and conferences with department chiefs are the major concerns of these city managers. Direct citizen contact and inspecting and supervising line municipal activities and personnel problems take up a much smaller percentage of a large-city manager's time. This is no doubt due to the fact that managers in these communities have sizable staffs to handle the more specialized functions of municipal management, which permits the manager to concentrate on the broader policy issues of municipal administration. In these cities, managers frequently are older, have college degrees at least, and are normally men with broad administrative experience inside and outside of government. Their work, salaries, and backgrounds compare favorably with those of high-level federal civil servants and corporation executives. Their job activities are much less routine and considerably more policy oriented. One characteristic large-city manager in a city of five hundred thousand people estimated his weekly distribution of time among various municipal activities as shown in Table 8.

TABLE 8
Typical Time Distribution of a Large City Manager

	Weekly %
Speaking with Citizens by Phone or in the Office	10
Conferences with Council or Department Heads	30
Planning Current and Future Activities	15
Handling Correspondence and Preparing Reports	15
Inspecting or Supervising Municipal Activities	5
Intergovernmental Work (with State and Federal Agencies)	10
Personnel/Labor Relations Work	5
Public Relations	10

At the other end of the spectrum, in the very smallest cities of fewer than ten or fifteen thousand people, managers frequently operate with small staffs and limited resources; therefore, they must normally deal directly with the immediate line operations of municipal government. When and how the water is pumped, fires put out, waste removed are the immediate issues of the small-town manager's daily occupational life. He has little in the way of staff assistance to supervise these line jobs, and therefore his occupational world consists of greater attention to the routine details of municipal work that are part of any city's life, such as police, fire department, public works, and the like. Policy questions, planning activities, and conferences with council members play a lesser part in his work. One typical manager of a community of five thousand estimated the percentage of his weekly time devoted to various municipal functions as shown in Table 9.

TABLE 9

Typical Time Distribution of a Small Town Manager

	Weekly %
Speaking with Citizens by Phone or in the Office	25
Conferences with the City Council or Department Heads	5
Planning Current and Future Activities	10
Handling Correspondence and Preparing Reports	10
Inspecting or Supervising Municipal Activities	40
Intergovernmental Work (with State and Federal Agencies)	5
Personnel/Labor Relations Work	5

The in-between cities—the middle-sized cities and suburban communities—place perhaps the broadest range of demands on managers, mixing many responsibilities of both policy and line activities. In these communities it seems the manager must be the most ambidextrous kind of administrator. He is close enough to the citizenry and line operations of government so that he cannot totally avoid preoccupation with such responsibilities, and yet his municipality is large enough in terms of population and fiscal resources so that the work can never become simply routine. Thus policy issues, planning activities, and conferences with the city council occupy a considerable portion of his time. The necessity for him to be a generalist is indicated by the way one typical city manager of a suburban community of twenty-eight thousand people estimated how he spent his weekly time (see Table 10).

The Three Varieties of Modern City Managers: Careerist, Administrative Generalist, Local Appointee

A second important impression gained from examining the 1971 Maxwell Survey data—and it should be emphasized that our conclusions are impressionistic—is that there seem to be three general types of managers: careerists, administrative generalists, and local appointees.[13]

Careerist managers tend to view city management as a lifetime occupation. They frequently made their career choice in college or graduate school and started their jobs in city management after schooling or military service. Frequently careerists have studied public administra-

TABLE 10

Typical Time Distribution of a Suburban Manager

	Weekly %
Speaking with Citizens by Phone or in the Office	20
Conferences with Council or Department Heads	20
Planning Current and Future Activities	10
Handling Correspondence and Preparing Reports	20
Inspecting or Supervising Municipal Activities	15
Intergovernmental Work (with State and Federal Agencies)	5
Personnel/Labor Relations Work	10

tion and hold masters degrees in the field. They have served apprentice-ships as budget officers or as administrative assistants to city managers before assuming city manager posts in their late twenties or early thirties. More than any of the three groups, they view themselves as occupational specialists in city management and therefore identify most closely with the city management profession by attending its meetings, subscribing to (and even writing for) important administrative journals, and later in life assuming important responsibilities in the ICMA. Their careers in the field tend to be mobile ones. They seek out the exciting, challenging city management jobs that are considered professionally rewarding and attractive; one can infer from this that they aspire someday to hold a large city managership position. However, their dedication to their communities and their immediate job assignments, as well as the need to maintain a good professional image, does not permit careerists to move *too* often.

Careerists have stronger ties with national professional organizations than they do with local civic clubs. They tend to hold more memberships and leadership posts in the former than in the latter groups. They also tend to keep better abreast of the latest innovations in municipal management and are more inclined to implement these new techniques in their communities. Moreover, careerists are more likely to have friendships and frequent contacts with other city managers and are more aware of the work of the leading practitioners in the field, such as L. P. Cookingham, Carleton Sharpe, and Thomas Fletcher. As a group, in short, careerists have the deepest commitment to the city manager profession, are normally the best educated in the discipline of public administration, have the longest tenure in the city management field, provide the core leadership for the ICMA, and are the most concerned about enhancing the prestige and status of the profession.

Administrative generalists constitute the second and perhaps the largest category of city managers. They are normally men who have entered the city management profession laterally, from a kindred occupational

career—business administration or governmental service. Like the careerists, administrative generalists have attended college, but they are less
likely to have studied public administration in graduate school; after their
schooling, they may have engaged in one or two occupations before
entering city management which gave them broad administrative responsibilities similar to the executive talents required of city managers. For a
variety of reasons—chance, advice of friends, desire for public service,
financial opportunities—they took managers' posts, frequently in middle
age. While they may have numerous professional ties, their local ties were
probably stronger than a careerist's would have been when they took their
first city management positions. And although they may exhibit the same
dedication to their work and their new profession as careerists, administrative generalists do not see their long-term career horizons as necessarily
limited to the city management field. They may move out to another
kindred field in business or government if the opportunity or need arises, or
they may very well find city management a rewarding and worthwhile
career to pursue for the remainder of their working lives. In short, the
major difference between careerists and administrative generalists seems to
be that the former are upwardly mobile within professional boundaries
whereas the latter group tends to be horizontally mobile across the broader
spectrum of administrative occupations in business and public service.

The least cosmopolitan kind of manager, in terms of education and
executive experience, is the local appointee. He lives in a small town and is
frequently a hometown boy with a large number of friends and contacts in
the community. He has few professional ties other than perhaps membership in the ICMA. His strongest loyalties are directed toward the numerous
local civic clubs and activities in which he probably participates. The local
appointee is a high school graduate and probably had a few years of
college at a local state university. If he ever left his community other than
for college, it was for military service. He holds no serious professional
aspirations, viewing his community as the only place he would ever like to
live. Frequently he is an older man who took the manager's post because
no one else wanted the job, or because his friends asked him to take it, or
because of his political connections, or because he saw it as a fitting job
before retirement. He rarely attends ICMA conferences, and he identifies
little with the general profession of city management. Management
innovations, new administrative techniques, current professional ideas hold
little attraction for him; he functions in his public office very much as a
routineer—that is, an administrator who attempts to make little or no
change in the way things are done. In brief, unlike the careerist or
administrative generalist who is either upwardly mobile or horizontally
mobile, the local appointee shows no sign of any geographic or job
mobility whatsoever.

Summary

Contemporary city managers are a highly homogeneous group of individuals: white, male, Protestant, native-born Americans, middle-class, middle-aged, married, college educated, residing in medium-sized middle western or southern communities and devoted to the full-time public service occupation of municipal administration.

Compared to pre–World War II city managers, the modern city manager is younger, much better educated, works in a larger city, is more likely to be found in southwestern and northeastern suburban communities, is much less likely to have been trained as an engineer, and is earning a salary two to three times higher than did managers in the 1930s.

The size of the community—large city, small town, or suburb—tends to define the manager's responsibilities, particularly whether his job centers on policy issues or line functions or a mixture of both.

The city management profession seems to have developed an informal pattern of "careerists," "administrative generalists," and "local appointees." Probably between one-quarter and one-third of city managers could be classified as careerists; possibly half are administrative generalists.

5

Public Professionalism in Perspective: *City Managers, Career Diplomats, School Superintendents Compared and Contrasted*

> One looks for these rewards, first of all, in the understanding and respect brought to one's work by one's own colleagues—in the sheer professional comradeship they afford. This is true of many professions: it is to the colleague, not to the outsider or the client, that one looks for real appreciation.
>
> George F. Kennan
> "Diplomacy as a Profession"
> *Foreign Service Journal* (1961)

> City managers and superintendents of schools have, over the years, had many common interests and points of contact. With the growth of urbanization these have expanded and multiplied. They run the whole gamut from school safety patrols, police, common use of school buildings and park areas through more fundamental matters of city and school budgets, urban renewal, juvenile delinquency, housing, health and crime. The similarity of roles of the city manager and the superintendent of schools has long been recognized.
>
> Bert W. Johnson
> *Realities of Intergovernmental Relations* (1964)

To what extent do city managers possess the attributes of other public professional groups? To what extent do they differ from other groups?

From the perspective of the political behaviorist school of social scientists, there are serious questions as to whether or not managers can be classified as professionals. In their view, managers are akin to local politicians—more readily responsive to local political pressures than to professional ideals.[1] Many students of professionalism likewise see the city manager as failing to fit the classic pattern of a traditional professional group. Managers do not undergo prolonged apprenticeships and they lack both a clearly prescribed occupational expertise and a tight professional association with extensive requirements for admission and advancement and established standards of professional accountability, such as those normally associated with the more traditional professional callings of law and medicine.[2]

Should managers, therefore, be properly classified as professional? Or do their occupational characteristics prevent them from entering the select ranks of professionalism? This chapter endeavors to explore the nature and extent, if any, of manager professionalism by a comparison with two other prominent occupational groups of public servants normally considered professionals within the context of American society: career diplomats and public school superintendents. The choice of these two groups as a basis for comparison was quite deliberate. City managers, career diplomats, and public school superintendents all apply their specialized expertise in important public roles; they significantly influence public policy decisions in their respective spheres of government—diplomacy, education, and municipal government—and ultimately they are all held accountable to publicly elected legislative bodies for their actions. In short, their general public nature gives them a common identity that provides a basis for mutual comparison (lawyers and physicians are largely but not altogether private practitioners, which makes a comparison of city managers with those professional groups a great deal more complicated—a task at least beyond the scope of this chapter).

The purpose of the comparative approach presented in this chapter is to offer a broader insight into the nature and dynamics of the city management field, yet it should be made clear at the outset that comparisons between city managers and other groups of public servants are difficult and of questionable intellectual value. For although public servants like school superintendents may share many attributes of managers—both operate on the local level in significant appointed administrative roles—other groups of public servants, especially those at the state and federal levels, often reveal little resemblance to city managers. This is certainly the case with diplomats. Diplomats devote lifetime careers to working in the large-scale bureaucracy of the State Department, whereas city managers are free-lancers who can move more or less at will from city to city, or even in and out of the city management field altogether. Diplomats serve the nation, not a locality, and are oriented toward international rather than domestic matters. And if a manager must often be a jack of all trades in fulfilling his varied administrative duties, the specialization accompanying a large-scale bureaucracy compels the modern diplomat early in his career to concentrate his expertise in a much narrower area. The diplomat rises or falls in his profession not as an administrative generalist but as a recognized authority on more narrowly defined policy issues such as nuclear test ban treaties, Latin American trade matters, or Middle East peace issues.

Finally, even though diplomats are ultimately responsible to elected officials—the president and Congress—their work is remote from these elected representatives by comparison to that of city managers. The manager works almost daily with a city council and mayor; therefore political-administrative relationships are a far more direct and central problem for the manager and his staff.

If it is apparent from the outset that managers and diplomats occupy considerably different roles as public servants, then why bother to compare the two? Ultimately, the clear contrast between them can be ample justification in itself for undertaking such a comparison. An appreciation of the important differences between managers and diplomats may bring the unique qualities of managers as public servants into sharper focus. Moreover, in the process of using as yardsticks two quite different groups who are clearly accepted as public professionals in the context of American government, we will be better able to determine whether or not city management can be classified as a profession to any significant degree.

City Managers versus Career Diplomats

The American Foreign Service as a public profession is perhaps the antithesis of city management.[3] From many standpoints, diplomats are the polar opposites of managers. Let us examine some of the differences between the two groups.

Historic Development: A Grass-roots Movement versus A Legislative Fiat

City management, as we have seen, was a product of the ideological and material forces of the Progressive era—the rise of American cities, the popularity of business and corporate ideals, the Progressive reform movement, and the scientific management movement. The manager plan, as outlined in Chapter 1, was adopted by numerous communities, primarily after World War I and World War II.

Whereas city management grew up from the grass roots of American society, the American Foreign Service sprang into being through a single congressional act. The Rogers Act (1924) was the joint product of two dedicated men, Congressman John J. Rogers of Massachusetts, who worked for five years to produce the legislation in Congress, and Wilbur J. Carr, then director of the Counselor Service. In a single stroke the Rogers Act created a detailed charter for a career diplomatic service, designating permanent Foreign Service officers with grades, ranks, and titles. The act established the merit principle as a basis for personnel selection, instituted a system of competitive examinations, set up a retirement program, created a noncareer class of clerks, and offered adequate compensation based on rank (initially higher than federal service pay scales).[4]

Since 1924 Congress has determined the size and strength of the Foreign Service primarily through annual budget appropriations and legislation affecting standards for entry. The standards for entrance into the Foreign Service are now rather complex because of the number of special lateral entry programs that Congress has authorized over the years. Besides the basic career examination route enacted in 1924, the Foreign Service has intermittently been expanded by several lateral entry programs: the 1939 Reorganization Act, the 1946 Manpower Act, Section 517 of the 1946 Foreign Service Act, the Personnel Improvement Program (1951), the Wriston Program (1954–58), and the Continuing Lateral Entry Program (1958 to present).[5]

Social Composition: Administrative Generalist versus Diplomatic Careerist

The 1971 Maxwell Survey data seem to indicate that most contemporary managers are administrative generalists, moving horizontally across a rather wide spectrum of administrative careers in business and public service. By contrast, the American Foreign Service is largely made up of diplomatic careerists. Of the 3,507 Foreign Service officers in 1966, 2,303 entered by passing the career entrance examination. Most of the rest were lateral entrants, primarily from the Wriston Program (1954–58). Lifetime dedication to a single field of activity is, therefore, considerably more common than in the city management field.

As one perceptive observer of the Foreign Service has noted, lateral entrants into the world of career diplomacy face certain hazards:

> The lateral entrant faces a number of handicaps. He is a "loner" not entering as a member of a group as junior officers do. Often he has not undergone much pre-conditioning for a change that may come to him relatively late in life. The heavy odds are that he will be coming to work in one of the lower-status functional fields, since lateral entry normally is resorted to for the purpose of adding specialized skills not in adequate supply within the corps; these are the fields the examination entrants have shied away from.[6]

The unreceptive atmosphere to lateral entrants in the diplomatic service is largely attributable to the lateral entrants' violation of the career principle. These individuals inflate the upper diplomatic ranks and lower the promotion rate of junior officers. Also there is the fear that massive injections of lateral entrants tend to dilute the professional quality of the corps, at least from the perspective of the many career diplomats.

Besides being more career oriented, diplomats are drawn from a narrower social background than city managers. In 1966 44 percent were from the Northeast (23 percent of managers are from that region); 39 percent came from professional families as compared to 2 percent of managers; 86 percent had B.A. degrees (69 percent of managers); 33 percent had masters or more advanced degrees (27 percent of managers); and 92 percent had majored in liberal arts subjects (39 percent of managers).

The importance of the three major Ivy League schools—Harvard, Yale, and Princeton—for staffing the top echelons of the Foreign Service is apparent from the fact that of the seventy-two degrees held by officers in the two senior grades of the Foreign Service—currently seven career ambassadors and fifty-two career ministers—thirty degrees were taken at these three schools.[7]

Diplomats and managers clearly come from different strata of American society. The background of a diplomat tends to be professional, eastern, upper middle-class, and educationally elitist (although certainly less elitist today than prior to World War II). Except for the lack of women and blacks, city management seems to represent a broader spectrum of individual backgrounds.

Favored Educational Preparation: Functional versus Humanistic Learning

In city management, preservice training has traditionally consisted of acquiring highly specialized functional skills. In 1934, the Ridley-Nolting survey found that 77 percent of city managers had studied engineering in college. Today nearly one-third have had undergraduate engineering training. Increasingly higher percentages have had business and public administration educations. As Efraim Torgovnik found in his recent detailed analysis of city councilmen's preferences for managerial education backgrounds:

> Public administration was designated by the councilmen as the most desired educational specialty for a city manager candidate, a reflection of the responses of high-income councilmen, presumably businessmen. The field of business administration was considered the most popular second choice, and engineering ranked third.[8]

Diplomacy, on the other hand, has traditionally favored the liberal arts—history, literature, and politics—as the ideal preparation for its junior officers. In a 1966 survey of the American Foreign Service, 71 percent had majored in the humanities or social sciences as undergraduates. Only .8 percent had studied accounting; 1.7 percent, public administration; and 4.2 percent, business administration (in either undergraduate or graduate school).

Curiously, however, in recent years the training for managers and diplomats seems to be converging: managers are absorbing more humanistic and social science learning and diplomats are seeking out managerial skills. The turbulence of the cities has increasingly caused managers to turn to sociologists and political scientists for answers to complex urban social issues, while the proliferation of diplomatic operations overseas has caused a sudden recognition of the need for managerial expertise among diplomats. At present a strange reversal of roles seems to be occurring; managers are learning to become urban diplomats and international diplomats are acquiring managerial talents.[9]

Organizational Structure: Local Autonomy versus Bureaucratic Hierarchy

The formal organization of the manager profession represents the extreme form of decentralization; that is, the local city council selects its own manager. Managers, in turn, choose whether or not to belong to the professional association of managers (the ICMA). Few legal criteria deter a council from selecting the manager it desires, and, as is not true in the professions of law and medicine, no legal sanctions make membership in the ICMA a prerequisite for becoming a practitioner in city management.

The reverse is true in the case of diplomats. To become a practicing diplomat and exercise the privileges and responsibilities associated with diplomacy, a person must enter the bureaucratic hierarchy of the State Department. In Weberian bureaucracy, diplomatic offices are arranged in a hierarchical order; labor is specialized and responsibility divided. Authority derives from the office rather than from the individual holding the office, and eligibility for advancement is normally based upon personal achievement in the form of experience, education, seniority, and ability.

Unlike city managers, diplomats possess a strong sense of their collective service to society as a whole. The tight bureaucratic institution in which they serve provides a much stronger sense of their own organic unity.[10] Their representational function abroad offers them an unusual overview of America vis-à-vis the international environment. The voluntary professional association of managers, by contrast, renders many individual services to separate communities around the nation, but the pluralism of American municipalities prevents any similar sense of collective unity on the part of management practitioners. The manager's greater personal freedom from the bonds of professionalism allows him to adapt to particular local political environs. What managers gain in flexibility, however, they lose in collective conscience. Their relatively weak professional association permits a greater likelihood of professional inconsistency and irresponsibility (the "Mitchell Affair," discussed in Chapter 3, provides a case in point).

Professional Ideology: Ideological Diffusion versus Institutional Conservatism

The role of the city manager in post–World War II America has been the subject of considerable debate within the manager fraternity. Numerous ideologies have competed for acceptance as the best approach to management—neo-Taylorism, emphasis on policy leadership and human relations, the organic view, political realism, reform orthodoxy, and, since the mid-1960s, the new professionalism.

Diplomats, by contrast, have a much more unified view of their role in society. Their highly institutionalized formal structure, their informal organic unity, their traditional representational function, and their upper-class social homogeneity combine to foster a more cohesive ideology than the newer, open, more democratic management profession.

The classic diplomat generally views irrationality, weakness, and evil as constant in human nature and often considers the nation-state to be the highest form of political organization. He recognizes continual rivalry between nations and the need for political order as facts of international life and sees political negotiations, even military action, as essential for enhancing as well as protecting the interests of the state he serves. As Quincy Wright aptly observed, "Diplomacy is a supplement to, as well as, on occasion, a substitute for, war." The eminent British scholar of diplomacy, Sir Harold Nicolson, concluded that "the professional diplomist is the servant of the sovereign authority in his own country."[11] In brief, diplomats as a group tend to be politically realistic and institutionally conservative.

This perspective is even apparent in the writings of a group of young American diplomats who during the mid-1960s openly advocated a "new" or "modern" diplomacy. In fact, their recommendations as presented in *Toward a Modern Diplomacy* are hardly new or revolutionary. Most, if not all, of their recommendations aim toward reasserting effective institutional authority over foreign relations. Seemingly out of a sense of frustration, these Young Turks offer astute suggestions for developing better diplomatic relationships through stronger control and coordination of proliferating American activities overseas.[12]

Degree of Elite Control: Weak versus Strong Influence

Ever since the ICMA was organized in 1914, senior managers have helped to formulate the organization's goals and policies. Because of the ingrained tradition of local autonomy in the selection of city managers, however, the ICMA has repeatedly failed to enforce its own professional standards as embodied in the Code of Ethics; its organizational strategy has been more designed to attract than to discipline members.[13] Its most productive function has tended to be the generation and dissemination of professional knowledge in the city management field through its monthly journal, research publications, annual conventions, and periodic training conferences.

As in the classic archetype of Weberian bureaucracy, the Foreign Service elite has authority over the selection of junior officer candidates, passes on officer promotions, develops important foreign policy recommendations, and has wide authority over State Department operations at home and abroad. As Frederick Mosher and John Harr recently noted in their excellent study, *Programming Systems and Foreign Affairs Leadership,* resistance to instituting program budgeting (known as Comprehensive Country Programming System, or CCPS, in the State Department) in Foreign Affairs was largely led by career diplomats:

> . . . the CCPS group was increasingly confronted with hostility or apathy in the field and in Washington. Only a few ambassadors responded with enthusiasm. . . . Most ambassadors were neutral at best; some were hostile. Some agreed to a CCPS "installation" principally because it offered a way of getting an extra man on their staffs (Executive Assistant). Only a few of the senior Foreign Service officers were genuinely interested in the system.[14]

Moreover, the collegial background and hierarchical world of the diplomatic corps make the Foreign Service elite much more recognizable. This elite consists of those officers serving normally as ambassador, deputy chief of mission (DCM), country director, assistant secretary, deputy assistant secretary or those filling special posts like director general and director of the Foreign Service Institute. As Glen H. Fisher has written:

> Foreign Service society had a definite social structure. At the top is the career Ambassador and his wife. This is so by formal rank, and informally so, as this position implies recognition of the top qualities of the Service, the Ambassador's years of experience with exposure to the great variety of contingencies one must meet in the Service, and his repeated endorsements by the promotion system. He has direct responsibility for all official Americans in his country. The prestige of the United States rests on his shoulders at all times; he is the personal

representative of the President of the United States. Both the social ethics of the FSO society and the necessity for a clear chain of command require loyalty and deference to the Ambassador.[15]

While the 1971 Maxwell Survey of the city management profession found relatively few managers able to name the best practitioners in the field, a 1966 survey of diplomats found that most were able to rank quite precisely their individual first three preferences for the best men in the State Department.[16]

City Managers versus Public School Superintendents

If from several points of view diplomats are unlike managers, public school superintendents have a great deal in common with managers. Both are administrators of important community enterprises; both are at the beck and call of local boards; both face similar problems of general public apathy and wrath over local issues (frequently at budget time); and both earn a comparable remuneration for their services. As Bert W. Johnson has written, "The similarity of roles of the city manager and the superintendent of schools has long been recognized."[17]

Historic Development: The Need for Local Expertise in Education and Municipal Administration

Staunton, Virginia hired the first city manager, Charles E. Ashburner, in 1908 to solve its burgeoning municipal problems, particularly in the area of public works. Excessive legislative influence caused Staunton to turn to the council-manager plan, which effectively centralized administrative authority and responsibility in a single executive office.

The earliest public school superintendents were hired for similar reasons: to provide full-time administrative expertise within the educational system and to centralize authority and responsibility for educational administration in a single executive office. As early as the 1600s, colonial town meetings, school boards, and city councils directly supervised the construction of school facilities and the hiring of teachers. If there were any administrative duties to perform, a teacher or town official handled them. By the nineteenth century, however, the growth of cities and educational systems made such informal supervision impossible. As a special school committee of Providence, Rhode Island reported in 1828:

> . . . unless the schools be visited frequently and examined thoroughly and unless the school committees determine to give to

this subject all the attention and reflection and labor necessary to carry the system of education to as great a degree of perfection as the case admits, everything will be fruitless . Without this, every plan of education will fail and with it almost any may be made to succeed.[18]

Eleven years later Providence employed a superintendent, the second in the United States (Louisville, Kentucky had hired one in 1837). By the 1850s, most large American cities had full-time superintendents (St. Louis first hired one in 1839; New Orleans in 1841; Rochester, 1843; Columbus, 1847; Baltimore, 1849; Cincinnati, 1850; Boston, 1851; New York, 1851; San Francisco, 1852; Cleveland, 1853; Chicago, 1854; Los Angeles, 1854; Nashville, 1854; Detroit, 1855). Daniel E. Griffiths has summarized the evolution of the office of school superintendent as follows:

> Schools were first under the authority of local government. When the work became too onerous, committees or boards were appointed to manage the affairs of the schools. Along with population increase came a numerical increase in schools and an increase in the complexity of school problems—the latter added to by the influx of immigrants. As a result, those committees appointed to school affairs began to specialize in their duties. . . .
>
> The system of lay supervision was not to prevail, however, and all the cities eventually concluded that their systems must give way to a new order.[19]

Social Composition and Favored Educational Background: Administrative Generalist versus Educational Administrationist

While most city managers are administrative generalists, modern school superintendents are normally selected from within the educational ranks. In the most recent statistical study of public school superintendents,[20] 88 percent had been classroom teachers and 83 percent had served previously in some type of school administration position.

Generally the survey indicated a high correlation between the size of the educational system and the length of the superintendent's prior administrative experience. Superintendents of districts of one-half million population or more reported that 56 percent had previously worked as assistants, deputies, or associate superintendents, and 46 percent had held superintendency posts in other districts.

The educational backgrounds of city managers are quite diverse; the required training for superintendency positions, frequently specified by state or local laws, is by contrast more narrow and specialized. Ninety-six percent of superintendents hold advanced degrees beyond the B.A. (compared with 27 percent of managers), and 21 percent have Ph.D.'s or Ed.D.'s. Of those with advanced degrees, 95 percent hold degrees in some field of educational administration or supervision. Relatively few of 181 Ph.D.'s were earned in fields outside education: two were in science, two in law, one in philosophy, one in psychology. Studies of graduate curricula in educational administration further indicate that course work tends to be highly specialized and functional in content, including courses in fields such as educational organization, curriculum supervision, school finance, school law, school plant operation.[21]

Unlike the leaders of the diplomatic corps, an unusually high percentage of whom are Ivy League graduates, 72 percent of public school superintendents received degrees from public universities and only 2 percent from Ivy League schools. No data are available on superintendents' family backgrounds, though it is probable that, like managers and unlike diplomats, they come from a broad range of occupational and income strata.

Organizational Structure and Careerist Controls: Open versus Closed Shop

Managers are selected in most instances according to the immediate needs of individual municipalities. Public school superintendents, however, are drawn from a much narrower labor market, characteristic of a "closed shop." Promotions to superintendency positions are normally made from within the educational fraternity—to repeat, statistics show that 88 percent are former classroom teachers and 83 percent former educational administrators. The closed shop labor market is legally enforced, in most states, by the requirement for advanced educational degrees. To repeat some more statistics, 95 percent of superintendents have advanced educational degrees (21 percent with Ph.D.'s or Ed.D.'s) and virtually all degrees are in the field of educational administration or supervision. The necessary process of university certification sharply narrows the field of applicants and is an informal but very effective method of asserting careerist controls over the selection of superintendents.

A number of recent studies indicate that local school boards reflect a distinct conservative bias that frequently serves to reinforce professional control over appointments. As Greider and Romine indicated in 1965:

> Recent studies of school board membership show that the median age is about fifty, half are college graduates, and about two-fifths are high school but not college graduates. As a group, school board

members are drawn mostly from among owners or executives in business and industry and professional people such as doctors, dentists, lawyers, scientists and engineers.[22]

By contrast, as Efraim Torgovnik found in his well-documented 1969 study, councilmen in manager communities represent a diverse range of religious, educational, and financial backgrounds, reflecting somewhat more heterogeneity than most school boards.[23]

Professional Ideology: Role Confusion versus Role Expansion

The postwar period has seen considerable controversy over the societal role of city managers. Political scientists have even questioned the ultimate value of managers, particularly for large cities.[24] The necessity for public school superintendents has never really been challenged. For example, in the controversy at the New York City Ocean Hill–Brownsville school district in the late 1960s, the issue of centralized versus decentralized community control was debated but the need for a public school superintendent was never challenged.[25]

What has occurred is a dramatic broadening of the scope of the school superintendent's role and his influence in American communities. The pre–World War II school superintendent, like the city manager, was very much caught up in the cult of Taylorism. Commenting on his own study of education during this period, Raymond E. Callahan wrote in the preface to his book, *Education and the Cult of Efficiency:*

> . . . I was not really surprised to find business ideas and practices used in education.
>
> What was unexpected was the extent, not only of the power of the business-industrial groups, but of the strength of the business ideology in the American culture on the one hand and the extreme weakness and vulnerability of schoolmen, especially superintendents, on the other. I had expected more professional autonomy and I was completely unprepared for the extent and degree of capitulation by administrators to whatever demands were made upon them.[26]

This era saw the superintendent adopt the self-image of the businessman, as Daniel E. Griffiths has emphasized:

> The self-image of the superintendent as a businessman reached its maximum about 1930. The concept of the efficient, business-executive type superintendent was reinforced in the professional training courses which the leading universities offered at that time: Teachers College, Columbia, the University of Chicago, Stanford

University, and Harvard University. Teachers College was by far the
most influential since it had thousands of superintendents attending
classes.[27]

Today the typical school superintendent's activities are hardly confined
to the business executive role (no doubt a good many superintendents only
wish their jobs *were* limited to bookkeeping problems). His activities touch
almost every aspect of community life, particularly the most vital matters
regarding the preparation of the next generation of Americans. School
systems often lack funds and adequate buildings, and teachers are
frequently in short supply. At the same time, the general public and
various community groups expect relatively high standards of performance
from our mass educational systems, as is evident in the recent rash of
minority protests, taxpayer revolts, teacher strikes, and student sit-ins or
"stay-outs." The superintendent, possessing limited resources which are in
greater and greater demand, is very often caught in the middle of the cross
fire.

The impact of technology and the rapid growth of federal and state
assistance to school districts have made school administration an increasingly complex responsibility. Superintendents and their staffs now
confront difficult decisions related to a wide array of subjects: computer-
assisted teaching devices, new theories of staff relationships, collective
bargaining with employee groups, applications for federal grants,
programs to improve minority education, use of behavioral research in
curriculum development, not to mention the daily crises of parental
complaints and student misconduct. As Sidney P. Marland, Jr., the former
United States commissioner for education, recently summarized the
contemporary role of the school superintendent in the *Public Administration Review:*

> Broadly, the superintendent's role is one of reaching out, now, to
> those he serves—students, teachers, citizens—to find new accommo-
> dations for rational and creative discourse. He must learn to be
> adaptable during this time of stress and rise above the negative
> personal connotations. He must with greater compassion than ever
> struggle for the minority child and the poor. He must answer directly
> the demands for information, for accountability; he must learn the
> acts of political effectiveness. Furthermore, he must remain the
> humane teacher.[28]

Summary

The American Foreign Service can be characterized as possessing formal
bureaucratic hierarchy, a high degree of informal professional elite

control, and a fairly cohesive professional ideology. Public school superintendents are subject to formal decentralized control by local school boards,
informal professional control over recruitment, and broadening professional responsibilities in community affairs. City managers, by contrast, are
subject to the formal decentralized authority of city councils and to weak
professional attachments; in the last two decades, moreover, managers
have suffered from considerable "role confusion."

The highly structured diplomatic corps provides a uniform quality of
professional competence, frequently quite high, but its tight cohesive
structure can offer considerable resistance to organizational change. By
comparison, the city management profession is very loosely structured and
therefore provides very uneven standards of practitioner performance;
nevertheless, its elastic nature permits it to respond and adapt to local
political pressures. Public school superintendents occupy a middle ground.
With their formal decentralized control and strong informal professional
autonomy, they are adaptable to local political pressures, but at the same
time they are more insulated than managers from community political
demands.

Curiously, the higher the degree of institutionalization, the greater
seems to be the degree of uniformity in professional ideology. Rarely has
the Foreign Service questioned its professional role. Never has the State
Department drafted a diplomatic code of ethics, for most diplomats are all
too conscious of the views of their peers. The city managers, however,
have amended their code of ethics approximately every sixteen years.
Perhaps because their group norms are so amorphous and insecure,
managers must wrestle at more frequent intervals with the central values
of their professional role.

At the start of this chapter, we asked two questions: To what extent do
city managers possess the attributes of other public professional groups?
To what extent are they different? Ultimately, the answer seems to be that
each professional group has evolved to meet its own field's specific
demands for occupational expertise. The immediate needs of diplomacy,
education, and municipal government have shaped the formal and
informal structure of the Foreign Service and the professions of public
school superintendency and city management. Specific professional identity results, therefore, from present needs, and not vice versa.

So whether or not city management and other occupations can claim
professional status depends very much on how the practitioners see
themselves and how others see them. Most managers, perhaps for reasons
of prestige, like to view themselves as "professional"; many political
scientists, whose behavioral approach sees managers' actions as largely
shaped by local political pressures, perceive them as "local politicians";
and scholars of professionalism, whose professional archetypes are law and

medicine, believe that managers fail to fit many of the classic characteristics of a professional calling.

In several respects all these views are equally correct and incorrect,
because the very term *professional* is an open-ended one, always evolving,
relatively rather than absolutely determined, culturally defined, and
ultimately hinging on questions of value. The word itself takes on meaning
only within a specific historic and national context, and that meaning
depends, most of all, upon the vantage point of the beholder.

The Contemporary City Manager: *Some Perspectives on the Present Dilemmas and Future Directions of the Profession*

At 2:10 P.M. on May 7, 1970 (two months after the burning of the Isla Vista Branch of the Bank of America), I stood feet planted in the open doorway of the Yale Avenue Branch of the Bank of America in Claremont, California, and watched as 1,000 singing college protest marchers with picket signs hoisted aloft, red headbands, and Viet Cong flags rounded the corner of Harrison Avenue, about 15 abreast, proceeded forward down Yale, arms linked and closed up their ranks about 20 feet away while their leader began an anti-Cambodia, anti—Bank of America speech. I could see our police chief, in plain clothes, gauging the mood of the crowd from across the street. I knew our mayor was somewhere in the tight mass of emotion-charged young people, trying to reduce tensions. About 25 SDS types stood immediately in front of me, urging the marchers to enter the bank. Would the protesters maintain order, or would they enter the bank?

> Keith F. Mulrooney
> City Manager
> Claremont, California
> *Public Administration Review* (1971)

I remember trying to convince a mayor, who was smarter than I, that I would make the administrative decisions and he and the council would make the political decisions. This was a classy way, I thought, of telling him not to bug around with administration and to confine himself to the dirty area of politics. I never tried this argument again, when he said, "Oh! you mean you will handle the easy problems and the council and I will solve the hard ones." We may wear a non-political mask when we face the public, but it is a mask that hides one of the best politicians in town even if he is an anonymous one.

> William V. Donaldson
> City Manager
> Tacoma, Washington
> *Public Administration Review* (1973)

Today fifty-five million Americans live in communities governed by a complex relationship between an elected city council and appointed city manager. The acceptance and survival of this form of community government over the last sixty years is itself something of a remarkable achievement in American history, a feat which, as the first chapter of this study attempted to explain, was due in no small measure to the manager plan's remarkable ability to fulfill simultaneously both the ideological and practical needs of numerous localities across the United States. The growth of the plan, as the succeeding chapters have described, spawned in turn a new public professional, the city manager, an official appointed by the city council serving as the chief full-time administrator in local government. This final chapter will attempt to evaluate two important questions regarding the modern city manager: What are the current major dilemmas confronting the city management profession? In what direction can and ought the city management field move in order to strengthen the general effectiveness of the profession?

The answer to the first of these two questions draws together several themes discussed in earlier chapters as well as observations from contemporary empirical research on the urban management field. The answer to the second question hinges in part on the first: Given the present nature of the dilemmas facing the contemporary urban manager, where and how ought the management field to focus its energies in improving the effectiveness of the management profession?

At the outset, I must emphasize that I possess no special clairvoyant powers concerning the shape of things to come. My goal is simpler. As a student of the historic development of the urban management field, I wish to outline several major issues confronting city managers today and to cull from observations about the historic evolution of their profession some speculations about what should be done to develop the effectiveness of the urban management field in the years ahead.

Current Dilemmas Confronting City Managers: The Increase in Social Responsibilities

Anyone who reads a daily newspaper is all too conscious that America is rocked by change. To some, the rate of change may be alarming; others find it far too slow. Most people will agree that change is taking place at an increasingly rapid rate. And perhaps more than most people, public servants—at all levels of government—are conscious of the dimensions of change. Like the frontline troops on a battlefield, they frequently must face the first assaults of economic, social, and technological innovations. City managers are no exception. Today they—along with mayors, councilmen, and other local administrators—are found on the front lines of the battlefield of mounting urban crisis that stems from what some commentators refer to as the "temporary society."[1]

What kinds of new problems are local administrators facing? Let us examine several of these increasing social responsibilities as enumerated in

Dwight Waldo's recent essay, "Public Administration in a Time of Revolution."[2]

(1) *A revolution in science and technology.* Computers, Planning-Programming-Budgeting Systems (PPBS), systems analysis, and Project Evaluation and Review Technique (PERT) are but a few of the many recent inventions that local administrators are asked to understand in order to improve the effectiveness and output of local government. The application of these complex techniques is demanding more and more specialized expertise on the part of individual city managers.

(2) *A growing reaction against science and technology.* With the rapid growth of scientific and technological advancement has come a recognition that perhaps the world is becoming too impersonal, too artificial, and too mechanized. The flower children of the 1960s and books like Charles A Reich's *The Greening of America* or Theodore Roszak's *The Making of a Counter-Culture* reflect this reaction to the material, technological, and scientific society. While flower children may represent an extreme degree of disaffection, many citizens, to a greater or lesser degree, prefer the personal touch to the IBM-card treatment. City managers are thus confronted with a rising demand to deliver community service with more warmth, feeling, and personal concern.

(3) *A revolutionary increase in the means of violence and a growing commitment to the use of violence.* The political irrationality of our times, coupled with rising demands from various community interest groups, has fostered a growing commitment to violence as both a means and an end in itself by both minority and majority groups in America. Force is frequently spoken of and used to assert group prerogatives. In the midst of all the harsh rhetoric and actions, local administrators are expected to maintain community order, without themselves contributing to further violence.

(4) *The increasing fragmentation of social groups along lines of race, sex, age, and occupation.* The stability of the social order depends very much on shared bonds between all groups living within communities. Today, however, local officials are often confronted by hostile groups loudly demanding their own narrow self-interests. The substitution of "group interest" for "community interest" is a disturbing reality of modern American life.

(5) *The growing crime rate.* City managers must be quite conscious of the bewildering growth of crime and perhaps equally perplexed at their inability to find either the cause or the cure.

(6) *Revolutions in morals and values.* Dress, vocabulary, personal manners that were discouraged just a decade ago are now increasingly accepted. The reasons for this new permissiveness in society are complex and are no doubt related to the several items already enumerated. For local administrators asked to enforce uniform standards of law and justice, the wider range of permissible behavior presents a very real difficulty.

What recognizable norms exist and therefore should be enforced throughout the community at large? Do communities exist and, if so, to what
extent do individuals in them share the rights and obligations of
community life? The age-old issues of political philosophy have re-
appeared with alarming immediacy.

Special Problems for Urban Administrators Operating Under Council-Manager Government

If the problems outlined in the foregoing section affect most public
officials—if not most Americans—living and working in communities across
the United States, the city manager operates under a system of government
that all too often imposes special burdens on him. Council-manager
government makes it very hard for the manager to deal effectively with
the increasing difficulties involved in the governance and operation of
communities. Let us examine some of these problems:

(1) *The repeated ideological disputes over the pros and cons of
council-manager government are academic exercises that frequently force
managers into the untenable position of defending the council-manager
plan.* The historic tendency of reform advocates of council-manager
government has been to oversell the benefits of the council-manager plan,
typically stressing its ability to reduce taxes, eliminate waste, and end the
burdensome cost of local government. Critics of the plan periodically raise
the arguments that it overrepresents businessmen, underrepresents minorities, and rarely lives up to the claims of its advocates. Yet despite all the
heated political debate over the advantages and disadvantages of the plan
itself, no empirical evidence so far indicates that council-manager
government is any better or worse than other forms of municipal
government at coping with the ills that beset our urban centers. In his
impressive study, *1400 Governments,* Robert Wood found that the
expenditures and tax efforts for public services of New York suburbs vary
according to population density and per capita income, not according to
the political affiliation or structure of the municipal government. Robert
Dahl's classic study of New Haven, *Who Governs?,* while not concerned
with council-manager government, came to the similar conclusion that the
real social and economic issues affecting city life are, except for trivial
matters, basically beyond the control of the formal structure of city
government, no matter who governs. James Q. Wilson put his finger on the
obvious question in a speech at Bloomington, Indiana, some years ago:
"While who governs is an interesting question, an even more important
and more interesting question is what difference does it make who
governs." Wilson's conclusions, much like Wood's and Dahl's, is: "The

most obvious indicators of the quality of life in our cities—per capita income, median school years completed, home ownership, morbidity rates, participation in cultural activities—are not much affected by the form or functioning of city government."[3]

Wilson's words must be bad news for the ardent defenders and critics of the manager plan who see its success or defeat as a vital factor in decisions determining the quality of city life. But it should be good news for managers. Since the formation of the International City Management Association, managers have wisely sought to separate their interests in professional urban management from those of reform advocates of the plan. Many managers have known for some time, if only intuitively, that the debate over the pros and cons of manager government is something of an academic exercise and that the real rationale for their role is the simple fact that the manager plan exists as the accepted form of local government in one-half of all American communities with populations over five thousand.

Despite the many pressures by reformers to make managers defend the council-manager plan, ideological disputes over the plan itself only hinder a manager's ability to carry out the administrative responsibilities assigned to him by the city charter. Most managers recognize that their chief job is not to sponsor any particular brand of government but, as Bollens and Ries have emphasized, to introduce professional expertise at the local level in order to aid elected representatives in setting policy and solving problems.[4] As Don Price observed some time ago, managers are full-time professionals in the urban policy process who are more concerned with "doing the right things" than with "doing things right."[5] But the battles of local politics often drive managers into disputes over the relevance of the manager plan, and so to protect their own professional identity, they must repeatedly emphasize the separation of their professional interests from the debate over the merits of the plan itself. Needless to say, this is usually easier said than done.

(2) *The apolitical position assigned to the manager in council-manager government frequently obscures, and even at times inhibits, his vital contribution to the local policy-making process.* Both popular political mythology and the legal constraints written into most council-manager charters place enormous emphasis upon the division of work between the members of the city council as the chief policy makers in communities and city managers as the chief administrators within local government. The recent surveys by Efraim Torgovnik and Ronald Loveridge[6] of elected officials serving in council-manager cities only underscore the persistence of this sharp administrative-political dichotomy in the popular mind, even though the concept of scientific management that was so important to the manager movement before World War II has been largely discredited by Dwight Waldo, Norton Long, and other leading students of administration.

The able examinations of community politics in relation to council-manager governments by Harold Stone, Don Price, and Kathryn Stone, the studies of Gladys Kammerer and her associates at the University of Florida, the work of Aaron Wildavsky, and the case studies made by Frank Sherwood and David Greenstone all establish beyond question the importance of the role of managers in local politics and urban policy decisions. They show that the acid test of survival for managers is their ability to come to grips with the complex political realities of the communities in which they operate. Their strategic position in city hall, their full-time influence over the local bureaucracy, their control over the flow of information and policy recommendations to the city council force them willy-nilly into important political roles. Indeed, as David Greenstone showed in his study of San Diego, problems usually arise when managers ignore the political realities of community life.[7] Yet the fictional doctrine of the complete separation of administration and politics under manager government lives on and often works to obscure managers' valuable political contributions to community government. Indeed, the sharp dichotomy between politics and administration may at times inhibit managers from realizing the full potentialities of their important policy-making roles in community affairs.

Some political scientists, like the late Karl Bosworth, have argued that managers should drop the fiction of their neutrality altogether and openly become politicians and community leaders,[8] but managers know full well that they would soon be looking for other lines of work if they publicly proclaimed that they were indeed politicians. Managers therefore must continue to lead double lives, forced by necessity into being officially neutral while in fact they are scrambling for their share of political influence in order to achieve success for themselves and their programs. This built-in tension between the ideals and practices of council-manager government has made the relationship between managers and the elected council a perpetual subject of discussion almost from the inception of the manager plan, with no final resolution in sight. Perhaps the only way out of this dilemma is, as Clarence Ridley suggested sometime ago, for managers to recognize that they must work out these problems repeatedly on an ad hoc basis, case by case, city by city. This "solution," however, may be of little help to managers confronting the daily struggle of politics upon which their fortunes and programs so vitally depend.[9]

(3) *The middle-class, suburban biases of manager government compli-cate the manager's job in achieving broader cooperation with other units of government, particularly central cities.* Most council-manager cities are predominately upper-class or middle-class in character. In ranking 74 Chicago suburbs in terms of housing value (a good indicator of social class), Edgar L. Sherbenou found that 18 of the 20 cities with the highest home values had the manager plan and none of the 31 cities with the lowest

home values had it.[10] Similarly, in a broader national sample of 300 suburbs in 25 large metropolitan areas, Schnore and Alford showed that, in comparison with other forms of urban government, council-manager governments were likely to have a smaller proportion of nonwhites and of foreign-born persons over sixty-five years old, with a larger percentage of people in white-collar occupations with higher levels of education. Manager cities tended also to be younger and growing more rapidly.[11] The data from these surveys frequently suggest, in short, that managers work in middle-class, white suburbs whose outlook, in the words of Robert Wood, represents "an ideology, a faith in communities of limited size and . . . a belief in the conditions of intimacy. . . ."[12] Although it is unfair to conclude that managers themselves have created or necessarily support the complex, fragmented suburban patchwork of metropolitan governments where people feel that good government must come in small packages, managers generally operate within an ethos that rejects solutions to urban problems that might demand broad cooperation between numerous localities in a given region. The fact that people move to suburbia in order to escape the problems of the central cities places grave obstacles in the way of managers—or for that matter any suburban local public official —who attempt to solve problems such as crime, pollution, fiscal imbalances, and racial segregation. Norton Long's study, *The Unwalled City*, paints a depressing picture of the results of the fragmentation of urban governmental structures. It shows the central city deteriorating to the status of "an Indian reservation" while the affluent whites who derive most of their income from the central city retreat to the suburbs in increasing numbers.[13] The autonomy of the suburban rings around the central city has contributed in no small way to the pathetic continuing decline of modern American urban life.

Deil Wright has demonstrated that managers are generally more responsible than most elected officials in attempting to work out cooperative agreements with other units of government,[14] but many of these temporary piecemeal agreements only appear to be solutions and actually serve to block more fundamental reforms in the system. The suburban middle-class ideology that is linked so closely with council-manager government sharply limits the range of choices available to policy makers in local government and works to direct managerial policy making toward decisions that often serve only to reinforce the segmentation of the urban scene rather than reversing the process. The irony that is apparently lost to the reform advocates of manager government is that the council-manager plan, idealized as a tool for improving local government, all too often lends itself unwittingly to the status quo forces of balkanization of the metropolis. Under these conditions, most managers will admit that they can individually do little to achieve broader urban integration.

(4) *The nonpartisan bias of council-manager government contributes to*

encouraging consensus politics which in turn inhibits city managers from securing broader community involvement in decision-making processes. Eighty-five percent of the twenty-three hundred manager governments are nonpartisan, and virtually all elect their city councils on an at-large basis; in contrast, less than half of the mayor-council governments have nonpartisan elections, and most of these select their councilmen either from wards or by a combination of at-large and district elections. Although nonpartisanship is by no means a necessary ingredient of council-manager government (manager government has worked just as well with partisan, ward elections), the same reform spirit that produced the manager form of government was responsible for fostering nonpartisan and at-large elections. Richard Childs, the father of the manager plan, for example, was an ardent supporter of both nonpartisanship and at-large elections. Today the Far West, the Midwest, and the South—the regions where the progressive reform spirit scored its greatest victories at the turn of the century—have the greatest percentage both of manager governments and of local nonpartisan elections.

The precise influence of nonpartisanship on the manager's ability to be an effective local administrator is hard to gauge because so little research has been done on nonpartisanship and its influence on city managers and also because it is hard to isolate the real effect of nonpartisanship in determining the way community decisions are made. But as Banfield and Wilson have pointed up,[15] the blurring of party lines does tend to produce greater homogeneity in local politics and also tends to place minority candidates, such as blacks, at a disadvantage in elections. For the manager and his staff, the consensus politics achieved through nonpartisanship may indeed be valuable in securing more rapid, more unified policy agreements from city councils as a basis for undertaking administrative actions, but it can also be detrimental to the manager by discouraging citizen influence and participation in community decision making. Under nonpartisanship, important disagreements over administrative action can somehow be more readily hidden and minority dissent less clearly voiced. One need not conclude, as did the National Advisory Commission on Civil Disorders (the Kerner Commission) in 1968, that city manager government compared to other forms of local government has "eliminated an important political link between city government and low income residents,"[16] but the nonpartisanship found in most city manager communities may help to obscure conflict over important issues and can at times reduce the input from minority groups into community decisions. It is hard to gauge the precise effect of nonpartisanship on decision making, again because of lack of research on the subject, but it is safe to argue that the consensus style of politics favored by most manager communities places a special premium upon the ability of managers to understand the complexities of community politics and to seek out the involvement of various dissenting groups who may not be well represented on the city council. Especially in heterogeneous communities, as Charles Adrian has suggested, the size of the city council might perhaps be expanded and district elections utilized to ensure improved representation of all factions of the community in council-manager governments.

(5) *While the central problems in community life have generally become less technical, recruitment of city managers still tends to favor the technical problem solver.* The city council members who hired Charles Ashburner as the first city manager of Staunton, Virginia in 1908 clearly recognized that the job required an individual with Ashburner's technical competence to deal with Staunton's public works problems. Improvement of roads, sewers, waterworks, and lighting were the chief tasks early city managers had to cope with, and, as most of these men were engineers, they were eminently capable of finding technical solutions to such problems. But today the job of the city manager is different. The problems he faces are mostly nontechnical and hence call for abilities much broader than those normally learned through engineering training. As Chapter 4 pointed out, the recruitment pattern of the management profession has reflected this shift from engineering-oriented to general administration–oriented individuals.

City councils, however, still favor city managers trained in engineering or public works. Even the administrative generalists hired as managers today are often men who have devoted a considerable portion of their time and training to technical problem solving rather than broader policy concerns. As Banfield and Wilson have written, ". . . the impression is unavoidable that managers as a class are better at assembling and interpreting technical data, analyzing the logic of a problem, and applying rules to particular cases than they are at sensing the complications of a human situation, or manipulating people, either through face to face contacts or through the media of commmunications."[17] Although there is no reason to conclude that men cannot or do not broaden their capabilities and outlook in fulfilling the new and changing demands of their work, the manager profession could nevertheless profit by drawing a substantially greater precentage of its membership from the humanistic disciplines of political science, history, economics, and sociology. In particular the profession should look for persons with broader insights into the nature, functions, and complexities of modern urban life and persons with less affinity for applying technical solutions to what are fundamentally nontechnical problems. These qualities are not easy traits to learn, if they can be learned at all, but given the kinds of issues confronting modern American communities, one senses that much of the present preparation of city managers is inadequate.

(6) *The inadequacies in the preparation of city managers—and of most public service leaders—are to a large extent a function of the inadequacies*

of college and university education for the public service. A few institutions of higher education—notably Harvard, Princeton, the University of Michigan, Syracuse, the University of Pennsylvania, the University of Southern California, and the University of Kansas—have for some time made significant efforts to train men and women for the public service. Until recently, however, most schools have had very few specific training programs for government service, with the result that in the last generation the demand for capable leadership in government at all levels has far outstripped the capacity of most schools to produce such leaders. In part the lack of qualified candidates for the public service is attributable to the increasingly segmented structure of universities. As Frederick Mosher points out, education for the public service has suffered for some time from the increasing specialization of disciplines and subdisciplines that have "tended to inhibit interdisciplinary and interprofessional study and to de-emphasize the connection and interdependence so vital to any breadth necessary in producing quality and qualified public service leaders."[18] Edwin Stene has noted that until recently many colleges have been unwilling to point out the options available to graduating seniors in the field of public service and specifically in city management.[19] Fundamentally, universities remain unable to decide what constitutes appropriate training for future public servants. Not only are public service jobs very different from each other, but also the complex nature of policy formulation itself, with its varied, often obscure, values, personalities, pressures, institutions, and sources of information and misinformation, almost defies the traditional, formal classroom approach to learning. The complexities of modern urban management are so great that, as William Donaldson wrote in a recent article in the *Public Administration Review*, city administration is comparable to lovemaking: it can only be learned by doing.[20]

The on-the-job-learning approach may have some merit, but one is tempted more to agree with Mosher's thoughtful view: "It is doubtful that there is any element in any evolving culture more significant for the nature of its public service than the educational system, both formal and informal, by which are transmitted its ethos, frame of reference and knowledge and partly through which these are changed and knowledge enlarged."[21] Unfortunately, Professor Mosher does not postulate just how higher education can more effectively produce future public servants for America. Norton Long, another leading scholar in the field, favors a greater emphasis on case studies, cross-cultural analysis, and the use of administrative histories. Long feels that such preparation would heighten students' sensitivity to the complexities of public administration.[22] Unquestionably, a high priority item on the educational agenda should be an increase in emphasis on the problems of public service education and clarification of the best ways to teach students how to carry out the responsibilities of administrative positions.

(7) *Although the ICMA has made many impressive reforms in outlook and structure during the last decade, the managers' professional association will remain a relatively weak voluntary association which requires continuing efforts to forge links between managers and scholars, federal agencies, and other groups working in the urban field.* The new look exhibited by the ICMA since the mid-1960s has been healthy for the urban management field. The organization has moved its national headquarters to Washington, D.C., staffed its ranks with new leaders, enlarged its research and training programs, and expanded its membership to include professionals other than city managers. In the light of modern trends in the city management field, the ICMA was certainly wise to give up trying to protect the early reformist ideals of council-manager government. Yet the organization should make considerably more effort to develop its research capacities by applying the skills of scholars around the nation to current urban issues such as pollution, crime, the influence of the media on local administration, the impact of public employee unions, and energy problems. In addition, managers trying to grapple with the complexities of intergovernmental relations at the local level should be made aware more promptly and thoroughly of developments in federal agencies that affect cities. And while there have been noteworthy examples of ICMA collaboration with major public service groups working in the urban field, further ties and linkages need to be established with the increasing array of private citizen groups concerned with the problems of our cities. To be sure, time, staff, and funds are limited in the ICMA as in all organizations, but more contacts with the world of scholarship, the federal government, and community-oriented private citizen groups would serve greatly to enhance the prestige and performance of city managers who look to the ICMA for professional leadership and education.

The First Priority for Urban Management in the Years Ahead: A New Self-image for the City Manager?

Many of the dilemmas confronting the urban management profession are too complex to be solved by the individual city manager or even by the government as a whole. In many cases, acceptable solutions are as yet unavailable. Government has never been able to reform people's racial attitudes, change the ideas of young people, or eliminate crime. These issues are parts of the fundamental moral questions besetting the United States in the twentieth century. Even if a unanimous American public suddenly decreed that something should be done, for example, to stop the use of hard drugs, the government knows very little about what causes individuals to use hard drugs; it knows even less how to alter the habits of millions of drug addicts. The government's efforts to stop the sale of liquor during the 1920s and to reduce smoking during the 1970s have been egregiously unsuccessful; indeed, Prohibition was not only wasteful but produced harmful results.

The individual city manager is the prisoner of a peculiar form of local government, the council-manager plan, and he must accept its reformist emphasis on the separation of politics from administration and its middle-class, suburban, and nonpartisan biases. Even if it were somehow determined that the reformist conception of manager government was clearly wrong and harmful to people, an individual manager could do little to alter council-manager government because these convictions are so deeply imbedded in the legal, political, and moral outlook of many communities that have adopted the manager plan.

What can and should be done? In this author's judgment, the greatest need at the present time is for the manager profession to sort out its own intellectual orientation and to develop a more coherent image of its functions and purposes on the modern urban scene. Most managers still operate, as they have since World War II, handicapped by an ongoing "identity crisis" about their purposes and goals in local government. Official ideology proclaims that they must be neutral administrators when in reality they assist city councils in dealing with important issues and hence occupy powerful policy-making positions. Official dogma drastically underestimates the manager's importance in community affairs, but those who claim that managers should become "community leaders" are equally mistaken, for city charters do not give managers wide enough political powers to play such an august role. As recent surveys by Ronald Loveridge and Efraim Torgovnik suggest, popular notions about council-manager government keep the political-administrative dichotomy alive and well in most manager communities: the manager's role is believed to be apolitical despite all the evidence to the contrary. Is the manager therefore condemned to a schizophrenic professional existence? Must he continue pretending to be a political eunuch when he is in fact the major power in city hall?

I believe managers could find a way out of this quandary by adopting a more coherent image of themselves and their purposes in local government. The new self-image I suggest would be patterned after the image of the professional diplomat. A diplomat in the classic sense is a professional with expertise and training which he brings to bear upon the highly political environment of international affairs in order to achieve workable agreements and mutual accommodations between nations for the benefit of both the nation he serves and its allies. A diplomat's duty is not to solve world problems with technical solutions but to engage in the continual process of negotiations with the more limited goal of attaining or maintaining peaceful relationships between countries.

The central issues facing city managers today are similar problems of human relationships and politics. Managerial talents and expertise are largely spent in shaping important policies with the city council, other government agencies and departments, and various community interest groups. Managers deal ultimately with people and solutions to human dilemmas, searching out accommodations to conflicts between groups and individuals with considerable amounts of misinformation, half-information, or no information at all. Frequently they must operate in a highly charged political environment. No pat answers are readily available, so managers must rely on an uncommon blend of expertise, creativity, fortitude, and political acumen just to survive. My argument is that such skills of human relationship and human understanding are best exemplified in the diplomat or statesman, who is both a professional and a skilled political realist trying to achieve an ideal world through negotiation and peaceful resolution of human conflicts. Modeling the city manager's role upon that of the diplomat would shift in several ways the traditional emphases of his primary duties in city life:

(1) The manager would be considered not a bureaucratic manager concerned primarily with good administration but a skilled professional dealing with the interrelationships and interactions between groups of people.

(2) Rather than looking for technical solutions to present problems, management would move to a "process orientation" that would stress the continual working out of relationships between individuals and groups in securing agreements over policy issues.

(3) From an emphasis on the logical interpretation of technical data and the application of rules, management would move toward a willingness to understand both the complex interplay of psychological, social, political, and economic forces at work in community life and the importance of being able to manipulate individuals to achieve peaceful adjustments among these complex forces.

(4) Managers would focus less on efficient, orderly routines of administration and more on continual bargaining with various groups inside and outside of government in pursuit of the public interest—in the broadest sense of the term.

(5) Rather than seeing himself as a neutral professional in local government, a manager would recognize that he is involved in the deepest political complexities and moral issues of our time. He must therefore gain an awareness of his limitations and potentialities in resolving these issues.

(6) Preparation for managerial positions would discard its technical orientation for a humanistic one and would strive to develop liberally

educated administrators, aware of the dilemmas of modern civilization and able to understand the interdisciplinary nature of their work and to use the approaches and skills of economics, sociology, history, and political science in resolving practical issues.

(7) Managers would rely less on the traditional techniques and issues of urban management. Instead managers should see themselves continually involved in the dilemmas of governance and strive to experiment with new and creative approaches which might help to involve more people in government—including some whose offbeat ideas are now overlooked but whose input may be vital in shaping effective administrative policies.

Changing mental attitudes is a difficult, complex, and occasionally impossible task. Nevertheless my argument is that managers should make their first order of business the project of developing a more unified and realistic view of themselves and their activities, a professional philosophy, so to speak, about their work that asks neither too little nor too much of their capacities as human beings in a unique and demanding environment. The image of the city manager as a professional diplomat on the urban scene with specialized skills in human relations, negotiation, compromise, and accommodation seems to strike an excellent balance between the practical realities of managers' jobs and the ideals toward which they can grow and contribute in a meaningful professional way in the development of their communities.

APPENDIXES

Appendix A

Important Dates

1894   The first annual meeting of the National Municipal League occurs on January 25. One hundred forty-five reformers gather in Philadelphia, Pennsylvania.

1899   The League's first Model City Charter is adopted. Haven Mason, first secretary of the League of California Cities, publishes "A Profession of Municipal Management" (see Appendix B).

1901   Galveston, Texas adopts the first Commission Plan.

1905   Professor Charles E. Merriam, University of Chicago, recommends as a member of the Chicago Charter Convention the appointment of a chief executive by the Chicago City Council.

1908   Staunton, Virginia adopts a city manager government. Charles E. Ashburner is selected first manager.

1910   Richard Childs unites commission and manager government in a proposed city charter for Lockport, New York.

1912   Sumter, South Carolina adopts the first official manager plan.

1914   Dayton, Ohio becomes the first major American city to adopt a manager plan. Colonel Henry M. Waite selected as the first manager of Dayton.

At the suggestion of Henry Waite, the City Managers' Association is formed at Springfield, Ohio. Eight of the thirty-one managers attend.

1915   The National Municipal League adopts the manager plan in its Model City Charter.

The Waite-Childs exchange at the National Municipal League Conference.

Harry A. Toulmin publishes *The City Manager : A New Profession,* sponsored by the National Municipal League.

1918   H. G. Otis becomes first full-time executive secretary of the City Managers' Association. Number of manager cities reaches 100.

1919   The association headquarters is established in New York City and the association begins publication of the *City Managers Bulletin* (in 1923 the title was changed to *City Manager Magazine* and in 1927 it became *Public Management*).

1922 John Stutz appointed full-time executive secretary of the ICMA. Headquarters moved to Lawrence, Kansas. Louis Brownlow elected ICMA president.

1923 Louis Brownlow's "Professionalism" editorial appears in *City Manager Magazine*.

1924 Association's name is changed to the International City Managers' Association (ICMA). Montreal ICMA Convention adopts the first Code of Ethics.

The Maxwell School, Syracuse University, under the leadership of Dr. William E. Mosher, establishes a city management training program (originally begun in 1911 at the Training School for Public Administration, New York City).

1927 Leonard White's *The City Manager* is published.

1929 ICMA headquarters is moved to Chicago. Clarence E. Ridley appointed executive director and Orin F. Nolting assistant executive director.

1930 Grants by the Spelman Fund establish the Public Administration Clearing House at the 1313 Center in Chicago. The ICMA becomes one of a cluster of ten public service organizations housed near the University of Chicago. Grants made for ICMA research and training programs.

1931 San Francisco adopts the first CAO (Chief Administrative Officer) city charter.

1934 ICMA Municipal Yearbook begins annual publication. Clarence E. Ridley and Orin F. Nolting publish *The City Manager Profession*. "Green Book" series appears.

1938 Revised Code of Ethics adopted at the Twenty-fifth ICMA Convention, Boston, Massachusetts. Number of manager communities passes five hundred.

1940 Publication of *City Manager Government in the United States* by Harold Stone, Don Price, and Kathryn Stone.

1945 Address on "The Job of the City Manager" is given at Harvard University by Clarence E. Ridley.

1948 C. A. Harrell's "Leadership Address" presented at the annual ICMA conference in Michigan.

Spelman Fund support ended for the ICMA and PACH.

1952   Revised ICMA Code of Ethics adopted. Number of manager cities passes one thousand.

1954–55   The Sayre-Bebout debate appears in the *Public Administration Review.*

1956   Orin F. Nolting becomes the ICMA executive director.

1958   Fiftieth anniversary of the first manager community is marked by publication of Clarence E. Ridley's *The Role of the City Manager in Policy Formation* and a special discussion of manager government in *Public Management* and *Public Administration Review.*

1961–62   The "Mitchell Affair," Newburgh, New York.

1964   *Long-Range Program for Urban Management Research* is published.

1968–69   ICMA headquarters moved to Washington, D.C. and Mark E. Keane named executive director. Number of manager cities passes two thousand. The Code of Ethics is revised. Name of organization is changed to International City Management Association. A new ICMA Research Series of books appears.

Appendix B

A Profession of Municipal Management

by Haven A. Mason

> This prophetic editorial by one of the founders of the League of
> California Cities, first secretary of that organization, first editor of
> the magazine *California Municipalities,* and longtime San Francisco
> city official appeared in *California Municipalities,* August 1899,
> pages 17–18. It provides a good reflection of reform sentiment at the
> turn of the century and offers a unique insight into the future
> development of the city management profession.

Why should there not be a distinct profession of municipal managers,
the same as we now have professions composed of lawyers, of doctors, of
engineers, of teachers, of accountants and others? We have come to look
upon municipal management as a matter of business, calling for the
exercise of sound business judgment and the appliance of strict business
principles. And yet when we come to consider it, it is a business peculiar to
itself. There is no other business concern like it in the commercial world.
And yet a great many people assume that anyone who has successfully
conducted any business undertaking can manage a city with equal success.
That this idea is a mistaken one is apparent when we consider the duties
that would fall to the lot of a "business manager" of a city. Were a city to
have a "business manager," we would expect him to be something of an
engineer; that is to say, he should have a technical knowledge of street
construction, the value of the different materials used therein for different
kinds of traffic and to be able to test the work done by the city's workmen
and contractors. Likewise he should understand sewer construction in all
its details, besides being familiar with the various methods of disposing of
the sewage and filth of the city. A city is also a constructor of buildings and
bridges, and whosoever exercises supreme supervision over the city's work,
should be capable of judging as to the fitness of all materials that have part
in such constructions.

Many cities now own their own water and lighting systems, and this fact
at once suggests that a city's "business manager" should know something
concerning the science of electricity, the science of hydraulics, the
operation of machinery. Otherwise, how would he know whether or not

such public works were being operated with economy, or whether the employees were competent or incompetent? Furthermore, he should be an accountant and be able to examine the books of the several municipal officers. He should have a fair knowledge of municipal law, understand the management of fire departments and be possessed of sufficient literary knowledge to see that libraries are properly managed.

These are, perhaps, the most essential qualifications that should be possessed by the "business manager" of a municipal corporation. Where is the man who possesses them all? The truth is we have not yet commenced to educate men to the profession of municipal managers. And it ought to be apparent to all who concern themselves in municipal affairs that it [is] nearly time to commence to fit men to occupy municipal positions. We have been assuming too long that any successful dry goods merchant or manufacturer could step from his present occupation and administer to the needs of a municipality with equal success. The assertion has been too often made that any business man who had made a success of private affairs is a sufficient guarantee that he would be equally efficient in the public service. This does not follow, and the assertion is no more true than to assert that a successful business man could successfully navigate an ocean liner. The management of a steamship is one business, the conducting of a bank another; the management of a city is still another. Municipal management should be a profession by itself.

Every city that receives and expends $50,000 annually ought to have a salaried business manager. Every private corporation that annually transacts that amount of business has one, and the same necessity obtains in relation to a public corporation. We complain because cities are mismanaged. Is it not so because we have so few who understand municipal business? We have theorists in abundance, but very few have practical knowledge. Up to this date there has been very little demand for expert knowledge in the conduct of municipal affairs. As soon as the demand exists, the supply will be forthcoming. Let one city place its affairs in the charge of a competent business manager and other cities will be demanding one also, for the improvement will be so marked that the citizens of other cities will take note thereof and demand a similar administration. Some city will become progressive enough before long to employ a "business manager," with an authority to conduct its affairs as broad as the manager of a private corporation has concerning its affairs. It may be necessary to import such a manager from Europe. In England and Germany there are municipal experts. Municipal management is the life work of a large number of people in Germany. Men are there trained to follow public employment. It would be an interesting experiment for a city to employ a professional manager, and it would be very likely to prove a successful experiment. Then ambitious young men would fit themselves for municipal employment and before long our cities would be managed by professional municipal officers instead of by professional politicians.

And when we require adepts to run our cities, our universities will establish a department to specially fit our young men to enter the new profession of conducting municipal business. Then it would be but natural to expect our municipal officers to hold diplomas from such institutions, just as we now require our school teachers to have certificates as to their ability to teach. And why shouldn't it be so?

Appendix C

What It Was Like To Be a City Manager in 1916 in San Jose, California

by Thomas H. Reed

> At the Forty-first Annual Conference of the International City Managers' Association in Breton Woods, New Hampshire, October 8, 1955, Thomas H. Reed delivered this colorful account of his personal experience as the first city manager of San Jose, California in 1916. Excerpted with permission from *Public Management,* December 1955, pp. 267–68.

Let me make a rapid inventory of the conditions I found in San Jose in 1916. The City's books were of the archaic single-entry type, which showed merely the inflow and outflow of cash. They provided no means of controlling the spending of appropriations or of measuring the cost of any function or activity. The annual budget was a crude piece of guesswork.

Purchasing was done by each department independently, in small lots, always from local vendors, with no adequate check on prices. Of course, the particular vendors who got their fingers into this juicy pie were those who belonged to the faction then in control of the city hall. All appointments had been made at the pleasure of the appointing authority with no attempt at any form of merit examination. There was no such thing as a city planning commission.

Turning to the service departments, the city's fire apparatus, it is true, had been motorized recently, but the two principal pieces were old fashioned steam pumpers to which three-wheel tractors, such as were then used in hauling heavy loads, had been attached in place of the horses. The firefighting force, moreover, worked a 24-hour shift six days a week. In this day of 48-hour weeks it is difficult to appreciate the effect on men of living together in comparative idleness 24 hours a day. They had the gossip propensities of an old ladies' sewing circle combined with the murderous inclinations of primitive man, and all their squabbles come across the manager's desk.

For health protection the city had a doctor part time, with no training for public health work. For recreation we had, aside from two or three downtown green spots, one large park in Alum Rock Canyon, seven or eight miles from the city limits. Its chief attraction was a bath house of imposing appearance. As might be expected, its architect had never before built a bath house. It had a glass roof over the pool and, consequently, algae on its bottom which caused customers to slip and slither. The slide, a tall one, was lined with terrazzo which abraded the knees and elbows of the customers and reduced the life of a bathing suit to a few hours, not to mention the chagrin it caused those sliders whose posteriors were unwittingly exposed to public view.

The public works department was capable of nothing but minor street repairs and some very sketchy street cleaning. Garbage and refuse were collected by a company of scavengers on a customer-fee basis. They had been a law unto themselves, collecting where and when it was convenient for them, while their appearance which corresponded with then current descriptions of Sicilian banditti frightened housewives out of their wits.

Our local street railway was very sick. Every time it cut its service in the effort to make both ends meet it actually sank deeper in the mire. It was owned by the Great Southern Pacific Railway but that organization had no intention of wasting any more of its resources than it could help on its weak subsidiary.

The police department was our weakest spot. The office and jail were in a vermin infested basement in the city hall, and the chief of police, who had been appointed only recently, was a red-faced, loud-voiced former butcher. Many of the members of the department had been appointed for political reasons. They had received no training except what they could pick up on the job from superiors as ignorant as themselves. The department as a whole was on good terms with the gamblers and bawdyhouse keepers. There were, as always happens, a few honest men in the department who would have liked to do a good job if they had known how and been given a chance, and they continued to be handicapped by their dead-wood colleagues.

You can readily understand that raising the every-day administration of the Prune Capital of America to a satisfactory standard would—under the best of conditions—have kept the manager's nose to the grindstone for many months. But other conditions were not wholly favorable. In the first place, the people had been sold only partly on the manager plan. Only four of the seven members of the council were fully devoted to it. This made the manager peculiarly vulnerable to the attacks of the politicians licking the wounds they had received in the charter campaign and getting ready for a comeback.

The big morning paper never ceased to harass me. It slanted the news. It attacked me editorially, and when the editor had a scurrilous jibe he did not care to print as the official view of the paper he would write himself a letter on the subject and sign it "Pro Bono Publico."

The relative ignorance of the public in those days concerning the techniques of municipal administration made it easy to ridicule with stinging effect the best things we did. As one example, we had some vacancies to fill in the police department. Professor Terman of nearby Stanford University was then gaining national recognition for his system of intelligence testing. We induced the civil service commission, set up under the manager plan, to bring Professor Terman to San Jose to examine several applicants for police jobs. The tests—the first ever applied in a civil service examination—proved very successful in getting the kind of men we wanted to appoint.

But one of the mental arithmetic questions ran: "If Berlin is 15 miles from Potsdam and a train runs 40 miles an hour, how long will it take to go from Berlin to Potsdam?" The brighter applicants had no trouble in answering the question, but the next morning's paper forcibly denounced the absurdity of supposing that a San Jose policeman needed to know how long it takes to get from Berlin to Potsdam. When this sort of thing goes on month after month even the conviction that one is right does not prevent the nerves from getting worn and frayed.

There was never a dull moment in Prunedom while I was manager. I do not suggest that I was ideally suited for the herculean task before me. I was young, inexperienced, impulsive, hot tempered, and addicted to making public speeches. My natural tendencies in this last regard were given too much scope by a bad feature of the charter which made the city manager not only the working but also the ceremonial head of the city government.

However, we did install a good encumbrance-type accounting system, institute carefully prepared budgets, carry on centralized purchasing with fair opportunities for competition, set up a civil service commission and a city planning commission, bring in and support a full-time professional health officer, acquire a competent city engineer, filter and heat the swimming pool water, and reorganize the police department under an experienced and honest chief.

I am not ashamed, therefore, that we made but one important public improvement, a new bridge, and that only because the old one fell down. Our immediate objective was the improvement of the day-to-day administration of the city and, with certain exceptions, we accomplished it. It was all we had time to do.

Appendix D

The Codes of Ethics: 1924, 1938, 1952, 1969

Association Code of Ethics (1924)

1. The position of City Manager is an important position and an honorable position and should not be accepted unless the individual believes that he can serve the community to its advantage.

2. No man should accept a position of City Manager unless he believes in the Council-Manager Plan of Government.°

3. In personal conduct a City Manager should be exemplary and he should display the same obedience to law that he should inculcate in others.

4. Personal aggrandizement and personal profit secured by confidential information or by misuse of public time is dishonest.

5. Loyalty to his employment recognizes that it is the council, the elected representative of the people, who primarily determine the municipal policies, and are entitled to the credit for their fulfillment.

6. Although he is a hired employee of the council, he is hired for a purpose—to exercise his own judgment as an executive in accomplishing the policies formulated by the council, and to attain success in his employment he must decline to submit to dictation in matters for which the responsibility is solely his.

7. Power justifies responsibility, and responsibility demands power, and a City Manager who becomes impotent to inspire support should resign.

8. The City Manager is the administrator for all the people, and in performing his duty he should serve without discrimination.

9. To serve the public well, a City Manager should strive to keep the community informed of the plans and purposes of the administrations, remembering that healthy publicity and criticism are an aid to the success of any democracy.

10. A City Manager should deal frankly with the council as a unit and

---

° The phrase "Council-Manager Government" means that form of municipal government in which the people choose a legislative body, be it called a Council, a Commission, or a Board of Directors, or something else, which employs a City Manager to exercise the administrative and executive functions of its city.

not secretly with its individual members, and similarly should foster a spirit
of cooperation between all employees of the city's organization.

11. No matter how small the governmental unit under his management,
a City Manager should recognize his relation to the larger political
subdivisions and encourage improved administrative methods for all.

12. No City Manager should take an active part in politics.

13. A City Manager will be known by his works, many of which may
outlast him, and regardless of personal popularity or unpopularity, he
should not curry favor or temporize but should in a far-sighted way aim to
benefit the community of today and of posterity.

Committee:

O. E. Carr, Dubuque, Iowa

Louis Brownlow, Knoxville, Tenn.

C. W. Koiner, Pasadena, Cal.

Frank D. Danielson, Hinsdale, Ill.

The City Manager's Code of Ethics (1938)

In order to achieve effective, democratic government, the council-
manager plan provides that municipal policy shall be determined exclusively by a legislative body elected by the people and that the administration of policy shall be vested in the city manager who, as administrative
head of the city, shall be appointed by and responsible to the council. The
International City Managers' Association is a professional organization of
city managers; its purpose is to increase the proficiency of city managers
and to aid in the general improvement of municipal administration. To
further these objectives, the Association believes that these ethical
principles should govern the conduct of every professional city manager:

1. No member of the profession seeks or accepts a position as city
manager unless he is fully in accord with the principles of council-manager
government and unless he is confident that he is qualified to serve under
these principles as city manager to the advantage of the community.

2. The city manager has a firm belief in the dignity and worth of the
services rendered by government and a deep sense of his own social
responsibility as a trusted public servant.

3. The city manager is governed by the highest ideals of honor and
integrity in all his public and personal relationships in order that he may
merit the respect and inspire the confidence of the administrative
organization which he directs and of the public which he serves.

4. The city manager believes that personal aggrandizement or personal
profit secured by confidential information or misuse of public time is
dishonest.

5. The city manager is in no sense a political leader. In order that

policy may be intelligent and effective, he provides the council with information and advice, but he encourages positive decisions on policy by the council instead of passive acceptance of his recommendations.

6. The city manager realizes that it is the council, the elected representatives of the people, which is entitled to the credit for the fulfillment of municipal policies and leaves to the council the defense of policies which may be criticized.

7. The city manager keeps the community informed on municipal affairs but keeps himself in the background by emphasizing the importance of the facts.

8. The city manager, in order to preserve his integrity as a professional administrator, resists any encroachment on his control of personnel, insists on the exercise of his own judgment in accomplishing council policies, and deals frankly with the council as a unit rather than secretly with its individual members.

9. The city manager handles all matters of personnel on the basis of merit. Political, religious, and racial considerations carry no weight in appointments, salary increases, promotions, and discipline in the municipal service.

10. The city manager curries no personal favors. He is the administrator for all the people and handles each administrative problem without discrimination on the basis of principle and justice.

The City Manager's Code of Ethics (1952)

To achieve effective and democratic local government, the council-manager plan provides that policies shall be determined by the governing body elected by the people and that the administration of such policies shall be vested in the city manager who shall be appointed by and responsible to the governing body. The purpose of the International City Managers' Association, the professional organization of city managers, is to increase the proficiency of city managers and to aid in the improvement of municipal government. To further these objectives, the Association believes that certain ethical principles should govern the conduct of every professional city manager.

1. No member of the profession accepts a position as city manager unless he is fully in accord with the principles of council-manager government and unless he is confident that he is qualified to serve to the advantage of the community.

2. The city manager has a firm belief in the dignity and worth of the services rendered by government. He has a constructive, creative, and practical attitude toward urban problems and a deep sense of his own social responsibility as a trusted public servant.

3. The city manager is governed by the highest ideals of honor and integrity in all his public and personal relationships in order that he may merit the respect and confidence of the governing body, of other officials and employees, and of the public which he serves. He believes that personal aggrandizement or profit secured by confidential information or by misuse of public time is dishonest.

4. The city manager as a community leader submits policy proposals to the council and provides the council with facts and advice on matters of policy to give the council a basis for making decisions on community goals. The city manager defends municipal policies publicly only after consideration and adoption of such policies by the council.

5. The city manager realizes that the council, the elected representatives of the people, is entitled to the credit for the establishment of municipal policies. The city manager avoids coming in public conflict with the council on controversial issues. Credit or blame for policy execution rests with the city manager.

6. The city manager considers it his duty continually to improve his ability and his usefulness and to develop the competence of his associates in the use of management techniques.

7. The city manager keeps the community informed on municipal affairs. He emphasizes friendly and courteous service to the public. He recognizes that the chief function of the local government at all times is to serve the best interests of all the people on a nonpartisan basis.

8. The city manager, in order to preserve his integrity as a professional administrator, resists any encroachment on his responsibility for personnel, believes he should be free to carry out council policies without interference, and deals frankly with the council as a unit rather than with its individual members.

9. The city manager handles all matters of personnel on the basis of merit. Fairness and impartiality govern the city manager in all matters pertaining to appointments, pay adjustments, promotions, and discipline in the municipal service.

10. The city manager curries no favors. He handles each problem without discrimination on the basis of principle and justice.

City Management Code of Ethics (1969)

The purpose of the International City Management Association is to increase the proficiency of city managers, county managers, and other urban administrators and to strengthen the quality of urban government through professional management. To further these objectives, certain ethical principles shall govern the conduct of every member of the International City Management Association, who shall:

1. Be dedicated to the concepts of effective and democratic local government and believe that professional general management is essential to the achievement of this objective by responsible elected officials.

2. Affirm the dignity and worth of the services rendered by government and maintain a constructive, creative, and practical attitude toward urban problems and a deep sense of his social responsibility as a trusted public servant.

3. Dedicate himself to the highest ideals of honor and integrity in all public and personal relationships in order that he may merit the respect and confidence of the elected officials, of other officials and employees, and of the public which he serves; believe that personal aggrandizement or profit secured by confidential information or by misuse of public time is dishonest.

4. Submit policy proposals to elected officials, provide them with facts and advice on matters of policy as a basis for making decisions on community goals, and defend municipal policies adopted by elected officials.

5. Recognize that elected representatives of the people are entitled to the credit for the establishment of municipal policies; credit or blame for policy execution rests with the member.

6. Make it his duty continually to improve his ability and his usefulness and to develop the competence of his associates in the use of management techniques.

7. Keep the community informed on municipal affairs; emphasize friendly and courteous service to the public; and recognize that the chief function of local government at all times is to serve the best interests of all the people.

8. Resist any encroachment on his responsibilities, believing he should be free to carry out official policies without interference.

9. Handle all matters of personnel on the basis of merit so that fairness and impartiality govern his decisions pertaining to appointments, pay adjustments, promotions, and discipline.

10. Seek no favors, and handle each problem without discrimination on the basis of principle and justice.

Appendix E

*A Sample Copy of the Nationwide Survey Questionnaire
Sent to a Random Sample of 11 Percent of the City
Management Profession, January 1971*

> *You are invited to participate in a national survey of the city
> manager profession. Please read this introductory letter, com-
> plete the questionnaire, and return it in the enclosed envelope
> by March 1, 1971.*

Dear Sir:

As part of a study of community leadership being undertaken at the
Maxwell School, Syracuse University, I am analyzing the characteristics,
attitudes, and other aspects of the city manager profession. You can make a
major contribution to this study by filling out the enclosed questionnaire. I
realize your time is limited and therefore the questions are phrased for
short answers. It should take no longer than twenty minutes to complete
the entire four-page questionnaire.

The survey results will be useful for scholars in understanding your
profession and for practitioners in the field of city management. The
results will be published in *Public Management*. Your individual answers
will be kept in *strict confidence*. No name is placed on the questionnaire,
and for this reason it is hoped that your response will be candid. In any of
your answers if you wish to make additional comments, feel free to turn
over the page and write out your thoughts more fully. Please answer all
questions or *as many as you can* and return this survey in the enclosed
envelope no later than March 1, 1971. Your assistance will be greatly
appreciated.

Sincerely,

Richard Stillman
NASA Fellow

Office of the Dean
Maxwell School
Syracuse University
Syracuse, New York 13210

SURVEY QUESTIONNAIRE OF THE CITY MANAGER PROFESSION

PART I: Personal and Community Information

1. Present age: _____ 2. Male: _____; Female: _____
3. Place of birth: _____
4. Are you married: _____; divorced: _____; widowed: _____;
   never married: _____
5. Your father's occupation: _____
6. Your job(s) before entering city management: _____
   _____

7. Please check your highest level of education: grade school: _____; high
   school graduate: _____; some college: _____; college graduate _____;
   some graduate school: _____; master's degree: _____; doctorate or
   LLB: _____.
8. If you went to college, what was:
   Your degree: _____ Major subject: _____
9. If you went to graduate school,
   Degree: _____ Subject: _____
10. Check any correspondence or in-service training courses that you have
    taken: budgeting or finance: _____; planning and zoning: _____;
    accounting: _____, law: _____; public works: _____; administration or
    management: _____; public health: _____; police administration;
    _____; fire administration: _____; personnel administration: _____;
    computers: _____.
    Other(s): _____
11. Check your political party preference:
    Democrat: _____   Independent _____
    Republican: _____   Other: _____
12. In what religious faith were you raised?
    Protestant: _____   No affiliation: _____
    Catholic: _____   Other: _____
    Jewish: _____
13. Do you live in the municipality you are managing?
    Yes: _____; No: _____
14. Please mark for each category the number (1, 2, 3) of civic or community
    groups that you belong to:
    Fraternal/Social _____   Cultural groups: _____
    Professional: _____   Hobby/Sports _____
    Veterans: _____   Political groups: _____
    Business groups: _____   Service groups: _____
    Country club(s): _____   Church groups: _____
15. How many offices do you hold in these organizations? (number)

16. What is the population of your municipality? (to nearest 1000)
     _____

17. Circle its geographic location: NE   SE   Midwest   SW   NW
18. Type of city: Central city:_____; Suburb:_____; Independent
     community:_____

PART II: Career Pattern and Work Characteristics

1. At what age did you first become a city manager?_____

2. How many communities have you served as city manager?_____

3. How many years have you served *this* city as manager?_____

4. How many years have you served *other* cities as manager?_____

5. Were you born in the community you now serve in? Yes:_____;
    No:_____

6. Where you born in the State you now serve in? Yes:_____; No:_____

7. Did you attend college or university in the State you serve in? Yes:_____;
    No:_____

8. At what point in life did you first want to become a city manager?
    (circle one)
    Earliest memories   High school   College   Graduate school
    Military service   In job after school   Other

9. From what source did you first gain an interest in city management?
    (circle one)
    Parent   Friend   High school teacher   College teacher
    Graduate school teacher   Employer   Other

10. Check the *principal* reason you first sought a city manager's position:
    Vocational interest:_____   Offered the position:_____
    Career development:_____   Advice of friends:_____
    Desire for public   Desire to help the city:____
       service:_____   Desire for more
    Other(s):_____   remuneration:_____

11. Check the *principal* reason in your opinion you were selected as city
    manager:
    Your experience in administration:_____
    Your experience in planning/renewal:_____
    Your experience in finance/budgeting:_____
    You federal/state experience:_____
    Personnel/labor relations experience:_____
    Your local ties:_____
    Executive experience:_____
    Recommendation of friends:_____
    Recommendation of former manager:_____
    Other(s):_____

12. Circle any statutory or charter requirements governing the qualifications for being the city manager in your city:

    Age limits   Good character   Residence requirement

    College training   Prior administrative experience   Other

13. What is the greatest source of *satisfaction* from your work?

    Public service:_____

    Financial rewards:_____

    Career development:_____

    Building the community:_____

    Being a community

        leader:_____ _____

    Public recognition:_____

    Other(s):_____

14. What is the greatest source of *dissatisfaction* from your work?

    Long hours:_____

    Low pay:_____

    Constant demands:_____

    Lack of public respect:_____

    Job insecurity:_____

    No time left for family:_____

    Political pressures:_____

    Other(s):_____

15. Check your *formal* manager responsibilities as specified *by the charter:*

    a) To supervise all or most parts of city government:_____

    b) To see that all laws and ordinances are enforced:_____

    c) To appoint, discipline, and remove according to law city employees:_____

    d) To prepare the annual budget and administer it after adoption:_____
    _____

    e) To advise council on the city's financial condition and other needs:_____

    f) To make reports or recommendations to council when requested:_____

    g) To control and/or make purchases:_____

    h) To keep the public informed on the city government operations:_____
    _____

    Other(s):_____

    Place an (X) to the left of the above function that requires during the year your most time and effort.

16. Is your manager's job: full time:_____; part time:_____; or combined with another municipal job (e.g. city engineer):_____.

17. Estimate the *average* number of hours you work per week:_____

    In an *average* week estimate the percentage (%) of your time devoted to the following:

    a) Speaking with citizens by phone or in office:_____%

    b) Conferences with council or department heads:_____%

    c) Planning current and future activities:_____%

    d) Handling correspondence and preparing reports:_____%

    e) Inspecting or supervising municipal activities:_____%

    f) Intergovernmental work (with states & federal agencies):_____%

    g) Personnel/labor relations work:_____%

    On the *average* how many evenings per week do you have to work?_____

18. How much direct staff assistance to you have? (Number)
    Secretaries:_____;   Asst. City Manager(s):_____;
    Administrative Asst.(s):_____;   Other(s):_____
19. Write the number of professional and technical journals you subscribe to for the following categories:
    Municipal/Administration:_____   Planning:_____
    Business/Trade:_____   Social Science:_____
    Engineering:_____   Other(s):_____
20. Please check the statement that you believe best represents the city manager's proper role in exercising community leadership as specified in the ICMA Code of Ethics:
    a) The CM should exercise frequent, aggressive community leadership:_____
    b) The CM should only occasionally and carefully exercise leadership:_____
    c) The CM should confine leadership to within city administration:
       _____
    d) The CM should confine leadership to aiding council on policy issues:_____
    e) The CM is not a community leader but primarily an administrator:_____
21. If you left your position in city management, what work would you prefer?_____
    _____

PART III: Your Thoughts on the City Manager Profession

 1. Check the statement that you believe *best* compares the city manager's work with other professional groups:
    a) City management is an established profession like law or medicine:_____
    b) City management is an established public profession like diplomacy:_____
    c) City management is a new public profession like city planning:_____
    d) City management is an emerging profession like computer science:_____
    e) City management is not a profession in any sense of the word:_____
 2. Check which statement you believe *best* represents the future of the city management profession:
    a) There will be more large cities and suburbs adopting manager plans:_____
    b) There will be more suburbs and middle-sized cities adopting the plan:_____

c) The total number of manager cities will roughly stay the same:_____

d) The total number of manager cities will slowly decline:_____

e) Professional urban management will be increasingly accepted but called by names other than city manager (e.g. Chief Administrator):_____

3. Most professional groups have a core of skills that are essential for the practicing professional man to master and utilize. Check the *three core skills* that you believe are essential for city managers:

   Budget/Finance expertise:_____

   Planning/Renewal expertise:_____

   Personnel/Labor relations:_____

   Public relations skills:_____

   Computer skills:_____

   Human relations skills:_____

   Ability to manage and control programs:_____

   Ability to develop new public programs:_____

   Ability to negotiate with community groups:_____

   Ability to build community support:_____

   Other(s):_____

4. Most professional groups tend to develop their own codes of ethics that express their values, ideals, and prescribed behavior. Check what you believe is the *most* important part of the City Manager's Code of Ethics:

   Giving community service:_____

   Providing community leadership:_____

   Acting rationally:_____

   Carrying out council's policies:_____

   Being friendly and courteous:_____

   Offering modern management advice:_____

   Placing the good of the community above your own personal good:_____

   Advocating unpopular positions that you feel are necessary:_____

   Handling all matters on the basis of merit, fairness, and impartiality:_____

5. Circle what you think is the *most* valuable training for city management:

   University Liberal Arts   Public Administration   Political Science

   Law   Business Administration   Engineering

   On-the-Job Training

6. Circle the idea/program which if adopted you feel would serve *most* to improve the quality of the city manager profession:

   Contracts for managers   Licensing managers

   Improved training programs   Career retirement program

   A better code of ethics   A stronger professional association

   Other(s):_____

7. Name the city manager you consider to be the *best* practitioner in the field: (past or present manager)_____

Notes

INTRODUCTION

1. Gladys M. Kammerer et al., *City Managers in Politics: An Analysis of Manager Tenure and Termination* (Gainesville: University of Florida Press, 1962), p. 83.
2. B. James Kweder, *The Roles of the Manager, Mayor and Councilmen in Policy Making: A Study of Twenty-One North Carolina Cities* (Chapel Hill: University of North Carolina Institute of Government, 1965), p. 31.
3. Aaron Wildavsky, *Leadership in a Small Town* (Totowa, N.J.: Bedminster Press, 1964).
4. Oliver P. Williams and Charles R. Adrian, *Four Cities: A Study in Comparative Policy Making* (Philadelphia: University of Pennsylvania Press, 1963), pp. 307–8.
5. David Greenstone, *A Report on Politics in San Diego* (Cambridge, Mass.: Joint Center for Urban Studies, 1962).
6. Frederick C. Mosher, *Democracy and the Public Service* (New York: Oxford University Press, 1968), p. 132.

CHAPTER 1

1. As quoted from *City Management—A Growing Profession* (Chicago: International City Managers' Association, 1957), p. 31.
2. For the author's distinction between the terms *council-manager plan* and *city management profession*, refer to the introduction.
3. Frederick Jackson Turner, "The Significance of the Frontier in American History," in his *The Frontier in American History* (New York: Henry Holt & Co., 1920), pp. 1–38.
    For studies on the background of Frederick Jackson Turner's writing refer to: Lee Benson, "The Historical Background of Turner's Frontier Essay," *Agricultural History* 25 (April 1951): 59–61; as well as Chapter 1 of Richard Hofstadter, *The Age of Reform* (New York: Random House, 1955). Also more recently, Richard Hofstadter, *The Progressive Historians* (New York: Alfred A. Knopf, 1969), pp. 47–166, presents an excellent analysis of the life and thought of Turner. For other good studies of the period, see: Morton G. White, *Social Thought in America: The Revolt Against Formalism* (Boston: Beacon Press, 1957), and Henry F. May, *The End of American Innocence* (New York: Alfred A. Knopf, 1959). A good statistical review of the growth of late nineteenth-century urbanism is found in U.S. National Resources Committee, *Urban Government* (Washington: U.S. Government Printing Office, 1939), p. 181: "The aggregate urban population increased by 119 percent during the years from 1880 to 1890—rate of growth unequaled in any subsequent decade. . . . the number of cities increased by 37 percent—another record unequaled in later decades."
4. Lent D. Upson, *The Growth of a City Government* (Detroit Bureau of Governmental Research, 1931), p. 12. For a more general statement of the growth of local governmental functions during this period, consult: President's Research Committee on Social Trends, *Recent Social Trends in the United States* (New York: McGraw-Hill, 1933), Chap. 25, and Carroll H. Wooddy, "Changes in the Functions of City Government, 1915 to 1929," *Public Management* 15 (January 1933):8–10.
5. David M. Potter, *People of Plenty* (Chicago: University of Chicago Press, 1954), p. 125.

Potter's book has several excellent essays that explore the effect of abundance on the American character.

6. Dwight Waldo, *The Administrative State* (New York: Ronald Press, 1948), p. 6. Samuel Haber, *Efficiency and Uplift* (Chicago: University of Chicago Press, 1964) is also a good general study of the ideas of business efficiency in Progressive thought.

7. Several early books on city managers exhibit much of this business and scientific-management thinking; refer particularly to Harry Toulmin, Jr., *The City Manager* (New York: D. Appleton & Co., 1915) and Chester E. Rightor et al., *The City Manager in Dayton* (New York: National Municipal League, 1919).

8. Rightor, *City Manager in Dayton*, p. 2.

9. Richard S. Childs, "The Theory of the New Controlled Executive Plan," *National Municipal Review* 2 (January 1913):80. Refer also to comments by Richard S. Childs, "Professional Standards and Professional Ethics in the New Profession of City Manager," *National Municipal Review* 5 (April 1916):195–210.

10. Hofstadter, *Age of Reform*, p. 9; in Chap. 5 Hofstadter presents a detailed contrast of Progressive thinking compared to that of the new immigrant to America.

11. Term coined in Edward C. Banfield and James Q. Wilson, *City Politics* (Cambridge, Mass.: Harvard University Press, 1963); refer particularly to Chap. 3, pp. 33–46.

12. Waldo, *Administrative State*, p. 17; Waldo refers to Herbert Croly, *The Promise of American Life* (New York, 1909), p. 7, as an example of a writer who exhibits these dual tendencies.

13. Waldo, *Administrative State*, p. 50; for a good sample of Taylor's thoughts on the application of his methods to government, read Frederick W. Taylor, "Government Efficiency," *Bulletin of the Taylor Society* 2 (December 1916):7–13.

14. Woodrow Wilson, "The Study of Administration," *Political Science Quarterly* 2 (June 1887):197–222.

15. Fred W. Riggs, "Relearning an Old Lesson: The Political Context of Development Administration," *Public Administration Review* 25 (March 1965):70.

16. Frank J. Goodnow, *Politics and Administration* (New York: Macmillan Co., 1900), p. 16. For variations on the same theme, see: W. F. Willoughby, *The Government of Modern States* (New York, 1919); John M. Pfiffner, *Public Administration* (New York: Ronald Press, 1935); and Luther Gulick and Lyndall Urwick, eds., *Papers on the Science of Administration* (New York: Institute of Public Administration, 1937). It must be emphasized that public administration as a distinct and developed field of study did not receive a great deal of recognition in academic circles until the 1920s. My point, however, is that many of the ideas were in the air by the turn of the century.

17. Woodrow Wilson, "First Presidential Inauguration Address," as cited in the *Congressional Record*, 63d Cong., 1st sess., 1913, 50:2–3.

18. The best history to date of the development of the National Municipal League is Frank M. Stewart, *A Half Century of Municipal Reform: The History of the National Municipal League* (Berkeley: University of California Press, 1950). See also Alfred Willoughby, "The Involved Citizen: A Short History of the National Municipal League," *National Civic Review* 59 (December 1969):519–64. The entire issue was a special seventy-fifth anniversary issue.

19. See either H. J. Bruere, *The New City Government* (New York: D. Appleton & Co., 1912), or Tso-Shuen Chang, *History and Analysis of the Commission and City Manager Plans of Municipal Government in the United States,* University of Iowa Monographs, 1st series, vol. 6 (Iowa City, 1918) for a detailed history of the early development of commission government.

20. *The Origin of the City Manager Plan in Staunton, Virginia* (City of Staunton, 1954), p. 11.

21. Ibid., p. 9.

22. Ibid., p. 12.

23. Ibid., p. 34.

24. Ibid., p. 12.

25. Ibid., p. 17.

26. Orin F. Nolting, *The Progress and Impact of the Council Manager Plan* (Chicago: Public Administration Service, 1969), p. 11.

27. For a short biographical sketch of Childs refer to John Porter East, *Council-Manager Government: The Political Thought of Its Founder, Richard S. Childs* (Chapel Hill: University of North Carolina Press, 1965), pp. 3–14.

28. Ibid. East's description of Childs's life makes it clear that it was natural for Childs to have a close identification with business and corporate ideals. He started his career as an advertising executive with the Erickson Company and became general manager of his family's firm, the Bon Ami Company; later he served as assistant to the president of A. E. Chew Company. Ultimately he served as executive vice-president of the Lederle Laboratories as well as director of the American Cyanamid Company. Childs's whole life was involved in one way or another with the business community.

29. *World's Work* 60 (May 1, 1931):3.

30. Don K. Price, "The Promotion of the City Manager Plan," *Public Opinion Quarterly* 5 (Winter 1941):564. Herbert Emmerich described Childs as an "inventor"; see East, *Council-Manager Government*, p. 80.

31. East, *Council-Manager Government*, p. 20; quoted from Richard S. Childs, *Civic Victories: The Story of an Unfinished Revolution* (New York: Harper & Row, 1952), p. 8.

32. Richard S. Childs, "Civic Victories in the United States," *National Municipal Review* 44 (September 1955):402.

33. Childs, *Civic Victories*, pp. 47–70.

34. Louis Hartz, *The Liberal Tradition in America* (New York: Harcourt, Brace & World, 1955), p. 240.

35. East, *Council-Manager Government*, p. 77. Interestingly, in Childs's advertisement for a city manager for Sumter, he stated, "There will be no politics in the job; the work will be purely that of an expert."

36. Willoughby, *Government of Modern States*, pp. 528–29.

37. Frederick C. Mosher, *Democracy and the Public Service* (New York: Oxford University Press, 1968), p. 71.

38. Harold A. Stone, Don K. Price, and Kathryn H. Stone, *City Manager Government in the United States: A Review After Twenty-Five Years* (Chicago: Public Administration Service, 1940), p. 27.

39. Ibid.

40. Ibid., p. 28.

41. *The City Manager Plan of Municipal Government* (Washington, D.C.: Chamber of Commerce of the United States, 1930) and *The Story of the City Manager Plan: The Most Democratic and Efficient Municipal Government* (New York: National Municipal League, 1934).

42. A. R. Hatton, "Pitfalls of Our Profession," *Public Management* 9 (March 1927):240.

43. Leonard D. White, *The City Manager* (Chicago: University of Chicago Press, 1927), p. 291.

44. For a short statement of the growing postwar separation between city managers and the intellectual community, refer to *Long-Range Program for Urban Management Research —A Policy Statement, 1964* (Chicago: International City Managers' Association, 1964).

45. Edward C. Banfield, *The Unheavenly City: The Nature and Future of Our Urban Crisis* (Boston: Little, Brown and Co., 1968), p. 31.

46. As quoted in Robert C. Wood, *Suburbia: Its People and Their Politics* (Boston: Houghton Mifflin Co., 1958), p. 74.

47. Ibid., pp. 69–70.

48. Ibid., p. 18.

49. William H. Nanry, "San Francisco Adopts a New Charter," *National Municipal Review* 20 (May 1931):259.

50. Charles R. Adrian, "Recent Concepts in Large City Administration," in *Urban Government: A Reader in Politics and Administration,* ed. Edward C. Banfield (New York: Free Press, 1969), p. 518.

51. Ibid., p. 522.

52. Edward O. Stene, "Historical Commentary—Mayors and Administrators," *Public Management* 55 (June 1973):6.

53. Ibid.

54. The National Municipal League's *Model City Charter,* although revised in 1925, 1933, 1941, and 1964, has kept the manager concept as its central feature.

CHAPTER 2

1. Alfred Willoughby, "The Involved Citizen: A Short History of the National Municipal League," *The National Civic Review* 59 (December 1969):522.

2. Article 1, 1915 City Manager Bylaws. This goal was later revised in the 1924 constitution to read: ". . . to promote the efficiency of City Managers and aid in the improvement of municipal work in general."

3. Quoted from an excellent study by Richard B. Vogel, "The Origin, Growth, and Development of the ICMA" (Ph.D. diss., University of Iowa, 1967), p. 16.

4. The City Managers' Association, *Proceedings of the First Annual Meeting* 1 (1914):15. The eight managers present at this first meeting included: C. E. Ashburner, O. E. Carr, D. B. Chappell, H. M. Hardin, K. M. Mitchell, K. Riddle, C. E. Ruger, and H. M. Waite. Seventeen of the thirty-one managers then in existence joined the organization in 1914.

5. Leonard White, *The City Manager* (Chicago: University of Chicago Press, 1927), p. 281.

6. Richard Childs, "Professional Standards and Professional Ethics in the New Profession of City Manager," *National Municipal Review* 5 (April 1916):195–210. Childs's articles continued to appear in the pages of reform magazines and infrequently in *Public Management,* but the contrast between his thinking and that of practicing managers was well evidenced in "An Editorial," *Public Management* 12 (February 1930):37, in which Childs urged managers to take public services "out of the area of private profit or private philanthropy and run those services at cost for the general benefit." Such "socialistic" doctrines must have seemed revolutionary to the pragmatic-minded managers.

7. *City Manager Bulletin* 2 (January 1919):2. A good indicator of the close ties the City Manager Association had with the Chamber of Commerce was that of the thirty-seven organizational subscribers to the *City Manager Bulletin* in 1920, twenty-two were various local chambers.

8. Vogel, "Origin of the ICMA," p. 39.

9. *City Manager Bulletin* 3 (November 1920):2.

10. White, *The City Manager,* p. 275.

11. *Proceedings of the Eleventh Annual Convention* (1924):73.

12. White, *The City Manager,* p. 278.

13. Statistics and data were drawn from an outstanding analysis of the subject, "A Report of the Committee on Curricula," *Public Management* 11 (March 1929):131–37. Also, for thoughts of the dominant leaders on the idea of manager training, see Chester Maxey, "The Training of City Managers," *National Municipal Review* 9 (March 1920):142–45; William E. Mosher, "Training for the Public Service," *Public Management* (April 1928):325–28; Thomas

H. Reed, "Training for the Public Service," *American Political Science Review, Supplement* (1930):173–79. For a good summary of much of this thinking on education for city management refer to either: "Final Report of the Committee on Training for the City Manager Profession" (Luther Gulick, Chairman), *Public Management* 13 (May 1931):157–59, or Clarence E. Ridley and Orin F. Nolting, *The City Manager Profession* (Chicago: University of Chicago Press, 1934), Chap. 4, "Training for City Managership," pp. 48–59.

14. Ridley and Nolting, *The City Manager Profession*, p. 55.

15. Thomas H. Reed, "Training for City Managership," in *City Manager Yearbook* (Chicago: International City Managers' Association, 1932), pp. 165–73. For one of the best debates between the traditional university point of view and professional administrationist thinking on educating public servants, see W. E. Mosher and Robert Hutchins, "Shall We Train for Public Administration? Impossible," *Public Administration Review* (March 1938):3. Charles E. Ashburner's pragmatic thoughts on university training for city management provides an interesting contrast in Joseph A. Cohen, "City Managership as a Profession," *National Municipal Review, Supplement* (July 1924):391–411.

16. *The Annals of the American Academy of Political and Social Science* 51 (May 1922).

17. Ibid., p. 102. There is much evidence that managers were well aware of other professional codes, particularly the Code of Ethics for Engineers. The first survey of city managers, taken by H. G. Otis and appearing in "City Manager Data," *City Manager Bulletin* 2 (April 1919):6–11, showed that 49.2 percent of the 118 managers were former engineers.

18. F. E. Danielson, "Letter to the Editor," *City Manager Magazine* 7 (January 1924):29–34 and C. A. Bingham, "Proposing a Manual for Managers," *City Manager Magazine* 6 (February 1923):19–20. Vogel, "Origin of the ICMA," stated that the code was drawn also from C. M. Osborn, "The City Manager's Ten Commandments," *City Manager Bulletin* 2 (January 1919):4, but there is little relationship between Osborn's "Command-ments" and the 1924 code. Osborn wrote with tongue in cheek; the 1924 code was meant seriously. Similarly, Childs, "Professional Standards and Professional Ethics in the New Profession of City Manager," *National Municipal Review* 5 (1916) was an attempt to require adoption of the official manager plan as a criterion for membership in the City Managers' Association. Childs's thinking was not apparent in the 1924 Code.

The brief public debate over the code at the 1924 convention centered on what to call the manager plan: "city manager plan," "commission-manager plan" or "council-manager plan." As H. G. Otis concluded: "The objection to calling it the commission-manager plan is well taken—that we do not want the publicity of the commission plan which in many cases is not the right sort. The original objection to calling it, the city manager plan, was that we were charged with being a duplicate of the German Burgomeister system where one man is the ruler—the autocratic idea of one man running things." *City Manager Magazine* 8 (March 1925):74–76.

19. White, *The City Manager*, p. 284. White also observed, however, that in his talks with several managers throughout the country during 1925–26 he found only one manager who referred to the 1924 Code of Ethics (ibid., p. 285). While the code may not have affected individual managers, certainly it did reflect the collective spirit of the managers' association at that time.

20. A number of modern social scientists have mistakenly viewed the 1924 code as a sample of the early managers' sharp differentiation between policy making and policy implementation; section 12 states that "no city manager should take an active part in politics." Perhaps in the minds of the reformers of the National Municipal League this clear dichotomy existed, but the managers, as active practitioners, were considerably more sophisticated and experienced men in community affairs. While many sought to be ideal apolitical practitioners, they were in fact deeply divided over the actual degree of political involvement in community affairs. From the very earliest manager conferences several saw themselves as activists, participating firmly and decisively in all phases of community life;

others preferred a more restrained role. Compare, for instance, the activist position of Harry H. Freeman, "Selling Government to the People," *City Manager Association Proceedings* 7 (May 1920):128, to the restrained role of C. A. Bingham, "City Manager in a New City," *City Manager Magazine* 7 (January 1924):15. For a good summary of the differing points of view, read White, *The City Manager*, pp. 171–231.

Perhaps section 12 of the Code of Ethics should be seen as a compromise between the factions of activism and restraint. Indeed, it used only the phrase "active part," which left room for managers to take a "passive part" in politics. In section 7 of the code, moreover, the manager is clearly recognized as being included in the community decision-making process: "power justifies responsibility and responsibility demands power." Essentially the code asked managers to take a professional role in community affairs, but it did not forbid the manager to engage in policy-making activities.

21. Danielson, "Letter to the Editor."

22. Ridley and Nolting, *The City Manager Profession*, pp. xi–xii.

23. "International" was added principally to recognize the growing number of Canadian city managers at the 1924 Montreal ICMA Conference.

24. Article 8, the 1924 ICMA Constitution.

25. "Editorial," *City Manager Magazine* 6 (January 1923):5. Compare Brownlow's professional conception of the organization with an earlier unsigned editorial (not Brownlow's) regarding the City Manager Association as having primarily an informational role: ". . . it is not a professional, technical society . . . it is not a propaganda organization . . . it will always be sort of a dynamo for generating . . . facts and statistics gathered from its members" (*City Managers' Bulletin* 4 [February 1921]:3).

26. This profile is drawn from the five major pre–World War II surveys of the city manager profession: "City Manager Data," *City Managers Bulletin* 2 (April 1919):6–11; Joseph A. Cohen, "City Managership as a Profession," *National Municipal Review*, *Supplement* (July 1924); White, *The City Manager*; Ridley and Nolting, *The City Manager Profession*; Harold A. Stone, Don K. Price, and Kathryn H. Stone, *City Manager Government in the United States: A Review After Twenty-Five Years* (Chicago: Public Administration Service, 1940).

27. Ridley and Nolting, *The City Manager Profession*, p. 88.

28. White, *The City Manager*, p. 150.

29. Seymour Martin Lipset, *The First New Nation* (Garden City, N.Y.: Doubleday & Co., 1963), p. 370.

30. White, *The City Manager*, p. 94.

31. Henry Oyen, "A City with a General Manager," *World's Work* 40 (1911):220–28. For other studies of Ashburner, refer to: Frederick Palmer, "Man Wanted," *Colliers Weekly*, May 27, 1922, pp. 7–8, and Louis Brownlow, "The First City Manager," *City Manager Magazine* 6 (July 1923):7–8.

32. White, *The City Manager*, p. 99.

33. Thomas H. Reed, "Trends in City Management," *Public Management* 37 (December 1955):268. For a similar statement by Reed, refer to Thomas H. Reed, "The City Manager Plan in San Jose," *Pacific Municipalities* 30 (November 1916):197–202. Reed's rational approach to community government was later synthesized in his major book, which sought to develop a generic science of municipal administration: *City Management* (New York: McGraw-Hill, 1936).

34. *Fifth Annual Year Book of the City Managers' Association* (1919):103. For an interesting account of Carr's colorful career as manager, refer to White, *The City Manager*, p. 116.

35. John Edy, "Management Practice in Berkeley," as quoted in White, *The City Manager*, pp. 323–34. Also refer to Edy's "Managerial Functions of a Manager," *City Manager Magazine* 9 (March 1926):52.

36. Beginning in the early 1920's, annual ICMA conventions held discussion panels on

administrative problems and management techniques of cities, frequently based upon population size. The practice is still continued at ICMA conventions.

37. For an excellent summary of the extensive early discussions on council-manager relationship held at nearly every annual convention, refer to White, *The City Manager,* pp. 171–231.

38. David Riesman, *The Lonely Crowd* (New Haven: Yale University Press, 1950). For an interesting and successful application of Riesman's theory to college students that tends to justify its similar theoretical application to managers, see Elaine Graham Sofer, "Inner Direction, Other Direction, and Autonomy: A Study of College Students," in Seymour Martin Lipset and Leo Lowenthal, eds., *Culture and Social Character* (New York: Free Press, 1961), pp. 316–48.

39. Dwight Waldo, *The Administrative State* (New York: Ronald Press, 1948), p. 51.

40. White, *The City Manager,* p. 274.

41. Barry D. Karl, *Executive Reorganization and Reform in the New Deal* (Cambridge, Mass.: Harvard University Press, 1963), p. 139.

42. Abraham Flexner, *Funds and Foundations* (New York: Harper & Row, 1952), p. 135. During the first two years the Spelman Fund assisted a number of university and private research endeavors concerned with public affairs. *The New York Times,* April 7, 1931, 20:1 showed that the distribution of its funds to that date included grants of $52,500 to the New York State Conference of Mayors for the study of municipal problems and training of employees; $16,000 to the New York City Welfare Council for the study of New York State public employment office; $330,000, the Brookings Institution; $330,000, the National Institute of Public Administration: $265,000, National Council of Parent Education; $330,000, University of Chicago; $170,000, Child Study Association of America; $144,000, Regents of the University of the State of New York; and $100,000, Child Study Fellowship Program.

43. M. R. Werner, *Julian Rosenwald, The Life of a Practical Humanitarian* (New York: Harper & Row, 1939), p. 142.

44. Vogel, "Origin of the ICMA," pp. 100–103.

45. Louis Brownlow, *A Passion for Anonymity* (Chicago: University of Chicago Press, 1958), p. 222.

46. *ICMA Annual Yearbook* 9 (1923):151.

47. Frederic Haskin (Louis Brownlow), *The American Government* (New York: J. J. Little & Ives Co., 1911).

48. "Editorial," *City Manager Magazine* 6 (January 1923):5.

49. For two excellent accounts of Brownlow's life, read his autobiography, *A Passion for Anonymity,* and Barry D. Karl, "Louis Brownlow: The Professionalism of Service and the Practice of Administration," in Karl's *Executive Reorganization,* pp. 37–81.

50. "Report of the Meeting of the Committee on Research," November 1, 1929, as quoted in Vogel, "Origin of the ICMA," p. 155.

51. For example: Harry Toulmin, *The City Manager* (New York: Appleton & Co., 1915).

52. To understand the close relationship in methodology, compare White's book with C. E. Merriam, *Four American Party Leaders* (New York: Macmillan Co., 1926). Both focus in detail on personal characteristics and leadership styles of a selected number of individuals.

53. White, "The City Manager, pp. 305–6.

54. Ridley and Nolting, *The City Manager Profession,* p. 38.

55. Ibid.

56. It is worth noting that around this same time the enthusiasm of independent scholars for generic studies of municipal administration seemed to be reaching its height. Refer to two major works: Thomas H. Reed, *Municipal Management* (New York: McGraw-Hill, 1936), and H. G. Hodges, *City Mangement* (New York, 1939).

CHAPTER 3

1. Charles E. Merriam, "Democracy and Management," *Public Management* 27 (January 1945):2.

2. Clarence E. Ridley, "The Job of the City Manager," *Public Management* 27 (September 1945):258–63.

3. Paul H. Appleby, "The Influence of the Political Order," *American Political Science Review* 42 (April 1948):281. Virtually all of Appleby's books stressed the idea that administration and political processes were essentially inseparable. See especially his *Policy and Administration* (University, Ala.: University of Alabama Press, 1949).

4. Herbert Simon, *Administrative Behavior*, rev. ed. (New York: Free Press, 1965), p. 20.

5. Dwight Waldo, *The Administrative State* (New York: Ronald Press, 1948). Both Simon and Waldo, particularly compared with earlier administrative scholars like Luther Gulick and Leonard White, were relatively rooted in the European intellectual tradition. Simon's writings reflected the ideas of logical positivism developed by Ludwig Wittgenstein and other early twentieth-century British empiricists. Just as the logical positivists sought to make a science out of philosophy, Simon strove to make a science out of administration. By 1945, ironically, in *Philosophical Investigations*, Wittgenstein was rejecting his theories of logical positivism, while at the same time in America, Simon adopted these theories as his gospel.

Dwight Waldo worked from a broader western philosophical tradition and analyzed the influence of the unique American ideological and material environment on administrative thought. In this respect Waldo's concentration on the national character as influencing the creation of the administrative state bears some resemblance to the work of pre–World War I German historians of statecraft and of a few American historians of national character such as David Potter, author of *The People of Plenty* (1954). While Simon's writing could be characterized as scientific, universal, and ahistorical, Waldo's *Administrative State* is historical, philosophical, and humanistic. Both men's ideas did a great deal to set the intellectual agenda for American postwar scholarship in public administration. Interestingly, both men's philosphical perspectives are very much symbolized by their present academic positions—Herbert Simon is a professor at the Carnegie Institute of Technology, while Dwight Waldo is the Albert Schweitzer Professor in the Humanities at the Maxwell School, Syracuse University.

6. Ridley, "The Job of the City Manager."

7. John H. Ames, "The Art of Management," *Public Management* 32 (January 1950):2–6. For similar statements, refer to George Bean, "The Future of the Manager Profession," *Public Management* 37 (January 1955):2 and Carleton Sharpe, "The Past a Challenge to the Future," *Public Management* 40 (December 1958):282–86.

8. Sixteen of these studies were published in companion volumes: *City Manager Government in Seven Cities* (Chicago: Public Administration Clearing House, 1940) and *City Manager Government in Nine Cities* (Chicago: Public Administration Clearing House, 1940).

9. Harold A. Stone, Don K. Price, and Kathryn H. Stone, *City Manager Government in the United States* (Chicago: Public Administration Clearing House, 1940), p. 243.

10. C. A. Harrell, "The City Manager as a Community Leader," *Public Management* 30 (October 1948):290–94. Actually Harrell had expressed some similar thoughts twelve years earlier in an "Editorial," *Public Management* 18 (April 1936):97. The activist role he advocated for managers compares favorably with the thoughts of Louis Brownlow on city management (refer to the previous chapter).

11. Herman G. Pope, "The City Manager as a Leader in the Administrative Organization," *Public Management* 30 (October 1948):294–97.

12. Don K. Price, "Listening in at the Manager's Conference," *Public Management* 32 (January 1950):7–9.

13. Clarence E. Ridley, *The Role of the City Manager in Policy Formulation* (Chicago: International City Managers' Association, 1958).

14. An interesting comparison can be made between the access to research funds and the output of scientific management literature in the 1930s at Chicago and the availability of research funding in the 1960s for community power studies. For a recent article on the direction of social science research grants, see Robert Reinhold, "Social Science Gains Tied to Big Teams of Scholars," *The New York Times*, March 16, 1971, 26:1.

15. Some of these books were: Warner E. Mills and Harry R. Davis, *Small City Government* (New York: Random House, 1962); Gladys M. Kammerer et al., *City Managers in Politics: An Analysis of Manager Tenure and Termination* (Gainesville: University of Florida Press, 1962); Oliver P. Williams and Charles R. Adrian, *Four Cities: A Study in Comparative Policy Making* (Philadelphia: University of Pennsylvania Press, 1963); Aaron Wildavsky, *Leadership in a Small Town* (Totowa, N.J. Bedminster Press, 1964).

16. Karl A. Bosworth, "The City Manager is a Politician," *Public Administration Review* 18 (Summer 1958):216–22. For a complete listing of the writings of political realists on the city manager, refer to the bibliographical essay.

17. *Public Management*, the house organ of the ICMA and a good indicator of the directions of city management thinking, devoted comparatively little space to the writings of the political realists. Their point of view received about as much attention as those of doctrinaire reformers like Richard Childs and members of the National Municipal League, who after 1915 had little influence on the manager fraternity.

18. Richard S. Childs, "The Enduring Qualities of a Successful Manager," *Public Management* 45 (January 1963):2–4. For the continuity in the older reform doctrines during the postwar decades, refer to John Porter East, *Council-Manager Government: The Political Thought of Its Founder, Richard S. Childs* (Chapel Hill: University of North Carolina Press, 1965), particularly Chap. 6; and Alfred Willoughby, "The Involved Citizen," *National Civic Review* 58 (December 1969):519–64.

19. In 1966 approximately 6 percent of the ICMA revenue came from *Public Management;* 17 percent from dues; 38 percent, training programs; 16 percent, the *Municipal Yearbook;* 13 percent, management information services; and 10 percent, other sources. In the same year, expenditures went toward: 5 percent, *Public Management;* 32 percent, training programs; 13 percent, *Municipal Yearbook;* 11 percent, management information services; 39 percent, general administrative expenses. The statistical breakdown on the types of members in 1966: 58 percent were city managers; 16 percent were cooperating members; 2 percent were affiliated members; 13 percent, junior members; 1 percent, honorary members; 10 percent, associate members.

20. For a good summary of the distribution of these research grants among universities, see Reinhold, "Social Science Gains."

21. *Long-Range Program for Urban Research—A Policy Statement* (Chicago: International City Managers' Association, 1964), p. 2.

22. For an excellent study of the leadership difficulties of the ICMA during the postwar decades, read Richard B. Vogel, "Origin, Growth and Development of the ICMA" (Ph.D. diss., University of Iowa, 1966), pp. 171–236. Taylorism restricted the vision of other scholars from the Chicago school. As Dwight Waldo has written, even the most creative administrative scholar of that era, Leonard D. White, wrote his famous historical series on American administration from the "POSDCORB perspective"; see Dwight Waldo, *Perspectives on Administration* (University, Ala.: University of Alabama Press, 1956), p. 59.

23. For more details on the internal organizational structure of the ICMA, refer to Vogel, "Origin of the ICMA."

24. ICMA, *Minutes of the Executive Board Meeting,* November 25, 1961; also the *New York Times,* January 25, 1962, 1:3 and March 30, 1962, 1:2.

25. Besides the Steiner study, *Long-Range Program for Urban Research*, during the early 1960s several other studies were undertaken that recommended a number of organizational reforms within ICMA: the Goals Report of 1961; the Hank Meyer and Associates Report of 1962; and the Gunter Staff Report of 1962.

26. Joseph M. Heikoff, *Planning and Budgeting in Municipal Management* (Chicago: International City Managers' Association, 1965); W. D. Heisel, E. R. Padgett, and C. A. Harrell, *Line-Staff Relationships in Employee Training* (Washington, D.C.: International City Management Association, 1967); Michael A. Stegman, *Variations in Property Taxes and Investment in Owner-Occupied Housing* (Washington, D.C.: International City Management Association, 1968); David A. Booth, *Council-Manager Government in Small Cities* (Washington, D.C.: International City Management Association, 1968); Efraim Torgovnik, *Determinants in Managerial Selection* (Washington, D.C.: International City Management Association, 1969).

27. For an interesting statement of Keane's more flexible approach to city management, read his article, "Policy Leadership and the Council-Manager Plan," *American City* 83 (August 1968):115ff. His thinking on the subject sharply contrasts with Ridley, "The Job of the City Manager."

CHAPTER 4

1. The statistics for this study were gained from a survey questionnaire sent to a national random sample of 11 percent (numbering 245) of American City Managers (providing a 5 percent ± degree of accuracy). The survey was conducted from the Maxwell School, Syracuse University, Syracuse, New York during January and February 1971. The author wishes to thank those managers who took the time out of their busy schedules to answer the four-page questionnaire. In particular, thanks must also go to three members of the manager fraternity who aided in developing the survey questionnaire: Carleton Sharpe, of Hartford, Connecticut; David Bauer, of Wethersfield, Connecticut; and Bruce Clifford, of Auburn, New York.

2. For an interesting discussion of women in city management, see Alva Stewart, "Women in City Management," *Municipal South* 12 (January 1963):20–22.

3. For an unusual article on a black city manager, see William R. Fuhrman, "Our Profession: Who We Are," *Public Management* 52 (May 1970):2. For comments by two black city managers on the racial problems in suburbia, read an article by Paul DeLaney, "Outer City: Negroes Find Few Tangible Gains," *The New York Times*, June 1, 1971, 1:2.

4. Only 13 percent were Catholics and 3 percent Jewish; among Protestant denominations, managers were, in descending numbers, Methodist, Presbyterian, Episcopalian.

5. For a more detailed statistical description of city managers' family backgrounds, refer to Community Studies, Inc., "Past, Present, and Proposed Research on the City Manager," unpublished paper (Kansas City, Mo.)

6. For another study of managers' local participation, see Gladys M. Kammerer et al., *Florida City Managers, Profile and Tenure*, University of Florida Public Administration Clearing Service, Studies in Public Administration, no. 22 (Gainesville, 1961).

7. The idea for asking several of these questions was based on the survey questionnaire used by John E. Harr in his excellent study, *The Professional Diplomat* (Princeton: Princeton University Press, 1969). Refer to the appendixes of his book for a sample copy of the questionnaire.

8. For an interesting comparison of the views of modern managers on their leadership in policy making compared to those of pre–World War II managers, see Patrick Healy III, "Should City Managers be Community Leaders?" *Public Management* 15 (July 1933):219. Healy surveyed 419 managers in 1933 and asked: "Should the city manager be a community leader?" He summarized the results by concluding, ". . . Replies indicate that the great

majority of managers prefer to remain in the background in determination of public policies." The 1971 Maxwell Survey results seem to indicate that modern managers tend toward a much more aggressive role in policy leadership.

9. For a good insight into the thinking of L. P. Cookingham, read Al Bohling, "Our Profession: The Dean Looks Back—And Ahead," *Public Management* 52 (May 1970):8–11, and in the same issue, a discussion with Mark Keane, "ICMA: Serving the Management Profession," pp. 17–21. For the ideas of Thomas Fletcher, refer to his article, "What is the Future for Our Cities and the City Manager," *Public Administration Review* 31 (January/February 1971):14–19. The prominence of these men is probably due to their length of public service in the field, their frequent appearances at conventions, their writings, and the training programs they have initiated for young men entering the management field.

10. Several good statistical surveys of city managers appeared prior to World War II, including: Joseph A. Cohen, "City Managership as a Profession," *National Municipal Review, Supplement* (July 1924):391–411; Leonard White, *The City Manager* (Chicago: University of Chicago Press, 1927), particularly pp. 123–40; and Harold A. Stone, Don K. Price, and Kathryn H. Stone, *City Manager Government in the United States* (Chicago: Public Administration Clearing Service, 1940), particularly pp. 53–76. However, the Ridley-Nolting study *The City Manager Profession* (Chap. 7) seems to provide the most detailed statistical information on managers of that era.

11. Definitions of geographic regions are rarely uniform; for the purpose of this study, however, the Southeast includes the traditional twelve Deep South states; the northeastern states are those running along the Atlantic coast from Maine to Maryland; the Midwest covers the area from Ohio to Nebraska; the Southwest extends from New Mexico to California; and the Northwest includes the Pacific Northwest plus Alaska. Hawaii and Indiana are the only states without manager government.

12. It is worth noting that the Ridley-Nolting study, *The City Manager Profession*, p. 96 found a difference in the percentage of time managers in large and small cities devoted to various policy and line functions; they failed to elaborate on the significance of their findings, however. More recently, Efraim Torgovnik, in *Determinants in Managerial Selection* (Washington: International City Management Association, 1969), found significant differences in the preferences for different abilities and backgrounds of city managers by city councilmen in various-sized communities; refer particularly to charts 5-3 (p. 40), 6-3 (pp. 48–49), and 11-3 (p. 92).

13. Unfortunately there have been few sociological studies of the manager profession that have attempted to classify manager "types." One attempt, however, was George Floro, "Types of City Managers," *Public Management* 34 (October 1952):218ff., which also appeared in Edwin O. Stene, *The City Manager: Professional Training and Tenure* (Lawrence, Kans.: University of Kansas Publications, 1966), p. 34.

Morris Janowitz, *The Professional Soldier* (Glencoe, N.Y.: Free Press, 1960), makes a useful distinction between the two types of military officer, "hero" and "manager"; for the manager profession, however, a classification based upon Robert K. Merton, "Patterns of Influence Locals and Cosmopolitans" in *Social Theory and Social Structure* (New York: Free Press, 1957), is perhaps a more useful basis for distinguishing types of managers in relation to the degree of cosmopolitan and local attachment.

CHAPTER 5

1. Refer to Karl A. Bosworth, "The City Manager is a Politician," *Public Administration Review* 18 (Summer 1958):216–22. For other statements of political behaviorists, refer to the bibliographical essay.

2. For two scholarly essays on the problems of defining professions, refer to the first two chapters by Everett C. Hughes, "Professions," and Bernard Barber, "Some Problems in the Sociology of the Professions," both in *Daedalus* 92 (Fall 1963):655–88. For a tight theoretical definition of a public profession, read Samuel P. Huntington, *The Soldier and the State* (Cambridge, Mass.: Harvard University Press, 1957), particularly Chap. 1, "Officership as a Profession," pp. 7–18. Leonard D. White's legalistic definition of a public profession appeared in his book, *The City Manager* (Chicago: University of Chicago Press, 1927), p. 272. For a broad definition, refer to Frederick Mosher, *Democracy and the Public Service* (New York: Oxford University Press, 1968), p. 106. For other writings on the subject, refer to the bibliographical essay.

3. In this context, the term *city management* is used to encompass the broad range of chief administrative officers in local government—including township managers, county managers, city administrators, business administrators, and chief administrative officers.

4. For a brief account of the historic development of the Foreign Service, see Richard S. Paterson, "The Foreign Service: Four Decades of Development," *Department of State News Letter* 34 (July 1964):3. Also Warren Ilchman, *Professional Diplomacy in the United States, 1779–1939* (Chicago: University of Chicago Press, 1961). For the rather remarkable story of Wilbur Carr, refer to Katherine Crane, *Mr. Carr of State* (New York: St. Martin's Press, 1960). George F. Kennan, *Memoirs, 1925–1950* (Boston: Little, Brown and Co., 1967) offers a fascinating story of the American diplomatic corps from 1925 to 1950 by one of its most renowned professionals.

5. John E. Harr, *The Professional Diplomat* (Princeton: Princeton University Press, 1969), pp. 147–50.

6. Ibid., p. 263.

7. Ibid., pp. 157–66 and 171–88. For a 1962 statistical profile of the Foreign Service, see John E. Harr, *The Anatomy of the Foreign Service—A Statistical Profile* (Washington, D.C.: Carnegie Endowment for International Peace, 1965).

8. Efraim Torgovnik, *Determinants in Managerial Selection* (Washington, D.C.: International City Management Association, 1969), p. 35.

9. The last chapter of John Harr's *The Professional Diplomat* argues for "A Managerial Strategy for the Future," pp. 323–50, whereas the 1971 ICMA (Green Book) text, *Managing the Modern City* (Washington, D.C.: International City Management Association, 1971) clearly recognizes an expanding "leadership and human relations role" for city managers; refer especially to pp. 77–133.

10. The sense of organic unity is well expressed in George F. Kennan, "Diplomacy as a Profession," *Foreign Service Journal* 38 (May 1961):24. I have never seen in print a similar statement by a city manager.

11. Quincy Wright, *The Study of International Relations* (New York: Appleton-Century-Crofts, 1955), pp. 158–59, and Sir Harold Nicolson, *Diplomacy*, 3d ed. (New York: Oxford University Press, Galaxy Books, 1964), p. 41.

12. The American Foreign Service Association, *Towards a Modern Diplomacy* (Washington, D.C.: AFSA, 1968), particularly pp. 55–57. For a shorter reformist statement, see John Doe, "Five Minutes to Midnight in Foggy Bottom: Reformers in the State Department," *Interplay* 2 (October 1968):15–17. The political realism and institutional conservatism of the State Department was perhaps best exemplified during the early 1950s in the clash between the old China hands and Senator Joseph McCarthy.

13. Refer to Chapters 2 and 3 of this book for specific examples.

14. Frederick C. Mosher and John E. Harr, *Programming Systems and Foreign Affairs Leadership: An Attempted Innovation* (New York: Oxford University Press, 1970), p. 205; and also described in Frederick C. Mosher, "Program Budgeting in Foreign Affairs: Some Reflections," in *Memorandum* (Washington, D.C.: U.S. Government Printing Office, 1968). Perhaps a typical view of PPBS by senior Foreign Service careerists is found in Ellis Briggs,

Farewell to Foggy Bottom (New York: David McKay, 1964), p. 29. Briggs makes caustic reference to "ravening bureaucratic termites" who "have chewed their way into the woodwork of Comprehensive Country Programming System, as the latest revelation of the professional planners is labeled."

15. Glen H. Fisher, "The Foreign Service Officer," *Annals of the American Academy of Political and Social Science* 76 (November 1968):79.

16. The list of the top fifteen ranked FSOs is published in Harr, *The Professional Diplomat*, p. 319.

17. Bert W. Johnson, "Realities of Intergovernmental Relations," unpublished (Arlington, Va., 1964), p. 1.

18. T. W. Higginson, *History of Public Education in Rhode Island from 1636 to 1876*, p. 168, as cited in Theodore L. Reller, *The Development of the City Superintendency of Schools* (Philadelphia: privately published by the author, 1935), p. 11.

19. Daniel E. Griffiths, *The School Superintendent* (New York: Center for Applied Research, 1966), p. 6. Griffiths has written one of the best accounts to date of the historic development of the office of school superintendent. Natt B. Burbank, *The Superintendent of Schools* (Danville, Ill.: Interstate Printers & Publishers, 1968) gives an interesting personal statement on the job.

20. These figures were drawn from an excellent statistical study of school superintendents (unfortunately now somewhat dated), the American Association of School Administrators and the Research Division of the Educational Association, *Profile of the School Superintendent* (Washington, D.C.: AASA, 1960).

21. American Association of School Administrators, *Professional Administrators for American Schools* (Washington, D.C.: AASA, 1960), p. 66.

22. Calvin Grieder and Stephen Romine, *American Education* (New York: Ronald Press, 1965), p. 379.

23. Torgovnik, *Determinants*, pp. 6–7.

24. The boldest attack appeared in Wallace S. Sayre, "The General Manager Idea for Large Cities," *Public Administration Review* 14 (Autumn 1954):253–58; for the reply, see John E. Bebout, "Management for Large Cities," *Public Administration Review* 15 (Summer 1955):188–95.

25. For a detailed account, see Maurice R. Berube and Marilyn Gittell, eds., *Confrontation at Ocean Hill–Brownsville* (New York: Frederick A. Praeger, 1969).

26. Raymond E. Callahan, *Education and the Cult of Efficiency* (Chicago: University of Chicago Press, 1962), ix.

27. Griffiths, *School Superintendent*, p. 31.

28. Sidney P. Marland, Jr., "The Changing Nature of School Superintendency," *Public Administration Review* 30 (July/August 1970):365–71; for a similar view, also see Burbank, *The Superintendent of Schools*.

CHAPTER 6

1. Warren G. Bennis and Philip E. Slater, *The Temporary Society* (New York: Harper & Row, 1968); also Frederick C. Mosher, "The Public Service in the Temporary Society," *Public Administration Review* 31 (January/February 1971):47–62.

2. Dwight Waldo, "Public Administration in a Time of Revolution," address originally delivered to the Capitol District Chapter of the American Society for Public Administration, Albany, New York, April 1, 1968 and published in *Public Administration Review* 28 (July/August 1968):362–68.

3. James Q. Wilson, "Problems in the Study of Urban Politics," a paper prepared for a

conference in commemoration of the fiftieth anniversary of the Department of Government, Indiana University, Bloomington, November 5–7, 1964, p. 2.

4. John C. Bollens and John C. Ries, *The City Manager Profession: Myths and Realities* (Chicago: Public Administration Service, 1969).

5. Don K. Price, "The Promotion of the City Manager Plan," *Public Opinion Quarterly* 5 (Winter 1941):570–71.

6. Efraim Torgovnik, *Determinants in Managerial Selection* (Washington, D.C.: International City Management Association, 1969) and Ronald O. Loveridge, *City Managers in Legislative Politics* (Indianapolis: Bobbs-Merrill Co., 1971).

7. David Greenstone, *A Report on Politics in San Diego* (Cambridge, Mass.: Joint Center for Urban Studies, 1962).

8. Karl A. Bosworth, "The City Manager is a Politician," *Public Administration Review* 18 (Summer 1958):216–22.

9. Clarence E. Ridley, *The Role of the City Manager in Policy Formulation* (Chicago: International City Managers' Association, 1958).

10. Edgar L. Sherbenou, "Class, Participation, and the Council-Manager Plan," *Public Administration Review* 21 (Summer 1961):131–35.

11. Leo F. Schnore and Robert R. Alford, "Forms of Government and Socioeconomic Characteristics of Suburbs," *Administrative Science Quarterly* 8 (June 1963):1–17.

12. Robert C. Wood, *Suburbia: Its People and Their Politics* (Boston: Houghton Mifflin Co., 1958), p. 18.

13. Norton E. Long, *The Unwalled City: Reconstituting the Urban Community* (New York: Basic Books, 1972).

14. Deil S. Wright, "Intergovernmental Relations in Large Council-Manager Cities," an unpublished paper prepared for presentation at the 1970 meetings of the Southwestern Political Science Association at Dallas, Texas, March 26–28, 1970.

15. Edward C. Banfield and James Q. Wilson, *City Politics* (Cambridge, Mass.: Harvard University Press, 1963), pp. 151–67. Also refer to: Charles R. Adrian, "A Typology of Nonpartisan Elections," *Western Political Quarterly* 12 (June 1959):449–58; Eugene Lee, *The Politics of Nonpartisanship* (Berkeley: University of California Press, 1960); and James Q. Wilson, *Negro Politics: The Search for Leadership* (New York: Free Press, 1960), pp. 41–44.

16. *Report on the National Advisory Commission on Civil Disorders* (New York: Bantam Books, 1968), p. 287.

17. Banfield and Wilson, *City Politics*, p. 174.

18. Frederick C. Mosher, *Democracy and the Public Service* (New York: Oxford University Press, 1968), p. 25.

19. Edwin O. Stene, *The City Manager: Professional Training and Tenure* (Lawrence, Kans.: University of Kansas Publications, 1966), p. 82.

20. William V. Donaldson, "Continuing Education for City Managers," *Public Administration Review* (November/December 1973):504–8.

21. Mosher, *Democracy and the Public Service*, p. 60.

22. Norton Long, "Politicians for Hire," *Public Administration Review* 25 (June 1965):119.

A Bibliographical Essay on the City Manager

Although leading nineteenth-century thinkers such as Weber, Durkheim, and Mill frequently wrote on the related subjects of occupations and vocations, our knowledge of professionalization has principally been developed through the work of twentieth-century social scientists. The best general study of the rise of professions in the western world is still A. M. Carr-Saunders and P. A. Wilson, *The Professions: Their Origin and Place in Society* (London: Oxford University Press, 1933). Several sociologists have more recently examined the subject, including Everett C. Hughes, *Men and Their Work* (New York: Free Press, 1958); and Amitai Etzioni, *Semi-Professions and Their Organizations* (New York: Free Press, 1969). Three volumes of scholarly journals have been devoted exclusively to the subject and contain several interesting articles: *Daedalus* 92, no. 4 (Fall 1963); *Annals of the American Academy of Political Science,* no. 51 (May 1922) and no. 297 (January 1955). For a short but excellent summary of ideas related to professionalism read Talcott Parsons, "Professions," *"International Encyclopedia of Social Science* (New York: Macmillan Co., 1968), 12:536–46. There have been numerous short articles on professionalism in various journals; Howard M. Vollmer and Donald Mills have done an exemplary task of editing many of these in one volume entitled *Professionalization* (Englewood Cliffs, N.J.: Prentice-Hall, 1966).

Social scientists have only recently begun to examine professions within the public service, and there are few general treatments of the subject. The best to date, winner of the 1969 Louis Brownlow Book Award, is Frederick C. Mosher, *Democracy and the Public Service* (New York: Oxford University Press, 1968). Refer particularly to Chapter 4, "The Professional State," pp. 99–133. Other general works are Corinne Gilb, *Hidden Hierarchies: The Professions and Government* (New York: Harper & Row, 1966) and Brian Chapman, *The Profession of Government* (London: George Allen and Unwin, 1959). For an excellent short survey of the subject, see York Willbern, "Professionalism and the Public Service, Too Little or Too Much?" *Public Administration Review* (Winter 1954):13–21. Studies of individual public professional groups within American government have been more numerous and several are of first-rate quality: Samuel P. Huntington, *The Soldier and the State* (Cambridge, Mass.: Harvard University Press, 1957); Morris Janowitz, *The Professional Soldier* (New York: Free Press, 1960); Herbert Kaufman, *The Forest Ranger* (Baltimore: Johns Hopkins University Press, 1960); Stephen K. Bailey et al.,

Schoolmen and Politics (Syracuse: Syracuse University Press, 1962); Warner W. Lloyd et al., *The American Federal Executive* (New Haven: Yale University Press, 1963); Don K. Price, *The Scientific Estate* (Cambridge, Mass.: Harvard University Press, 1965); and John E. Harr, *The Professional Diplomat* (Princeton: Princeton University Press, 1969).

For several excellent studies of the historical period in which the council-manager idea developed, refer to: Richard Hofstadter, *The Age Of Reform* (New York: Random House, 1955), as well as edited readings by the same author, *The Progressive Movement, 1900–1915* (Englewood Cliffs, N.J.: Prentice-Hall, 1963); Lorin W. Peterson, *The Day of the Mugwump* (New York: Random House, 1961); Frank M. Stewart, *A Half Century of Reform: The History of the National Municipal League* (Berkeley: University of California Press, 1950); Samuel Haber, *Efficiency and Uplift* (Chicago: University of Chicago Press, 1964); Barry D. Karl, *Executive Reorganization in the New Deal* (Cambridge, Mass.: Harvard University Press, 1963). The classic work on the historic development of American administrative thought is Dwight Waldo, *The Administrative State* (New York: Ronald Press, 1948).

The literature specifically on the city management profession and the council-manager plan is extensive but of uneven quality and therefore should be read selectively. To date the best book-length history of the subject is still Harold Stone, Don Price, and Kathryn Stone, *City Manager Government in the United States* (Chicago: Public Administration Service, 1940). It is a review of the results and practical operation of the city manager plan in several cities after the first twenty-five years. The book was sponsored by the Committee on Public Administration of the Social Science Research Council and based upon in-depth case studies published in companion volumes: Frederick C. Mosher et al., *City Manager Government in Seven Cities* (Chicago: Public Administration Service, 1940) and Harold Stone et al., *City Manager Government in Nine Cities* (Chicago: Public Administration Service, 1940). Unfortunately, no comparable study has been undertaken since 1940; therefore many of the facts and data are now more of historic than current interest. Both Leonard White, *The City Manager* (Chicago: University of Chicago Press, 1927) and Clarence Ridley and Orin Nolting, *The City Manager Profession* (Chicago: University of Chicago Press, 1934) provide ample material on early city managers. The former book presents an interesting qualitative analysis of these early professionals. Although the material is accurate and skillfully presented, the author was an ardent admirer of city managers and therefore writes with something less than a detached point of view. Nevertheless, both volumes give a reader a good portrait of what early city managers were like individually and as a group. An often overlooked but nevertheless excellent analysis of early city managers (the first one to appear) is found in Joseph Cohen, "The City Manager as a Profession" (undergraduate thesis, Harvard University, 1924), which later appeared as a supplement to the *National Municipal Review* (July 1924):391–411. The earliest studies of city managers tended to be reformers' tracts emphasizing the various advantages of the council-manager plan: Harry Toulmin, Jr., *The City Manager* (New York: D. Appleton & Co., 1915); Tso-Shuen Chang, *History and Analysis of the Commission and City Manager Plans of Municipal Government in the United States*, University of Iowa Monographs, 1st series, vol. 6 (Iowa City, 1918); Chester E. Rightor et al., *The City Manager in Dayton* (New York: National Municipal League, 1919); Robert T. Crane, *A Loose Leaf Digest of City Manager Charters* (New York: National Municipal League, 1923); Herman G. James, *What Is the City Manager Plan?* (Austin: University of Texas, 1917); J. W. Scroggs, ed., *The City Manager Plan* (Norman: University of Oklahoma, 1918); Joseph H. Quire, *The City Manager Plan Of Municipal Government* (Berkeley: University of California Press, 1916); Lent D. Upson, *The City Manager Plan of Government for Dayton* (Dayton, O. Bureau of Municipal Research, 1914); Lent D. Upson, *One Year of City Management in Dayton, Ohio* (Dayton, O.: Bureau of Municipal Research, 1915); *The City Manager Plan for Chicago* (Chicago: Chicago Bureau of Public Efficiency, 1917); Charles P. Taft, *City Management: The Cincinnati Experiment* (New York: Farrar and Rhinehart, 1933). Charles E. Mabie, ed., *City Manager Plan of Government* (New York: H. W. Wilson Co., 1918), although principally a debater's handbook featuring the major arguments pro and con the manager plan, is nevertheless one of the best anthologies of the earliest articles related to council-manager government. The book contains several interesting statements in opposition to the manager plan (which principally came from proponents of the commission form of government); see particularly pp. 209–36. Also worth careful examination is Clinton R. Woodruff, ed., *A New Municipal Program* (New York: D. Appleton & Co., 1919), an important document in the history of the leading reformers' transition from supporting of commission government to support of the city manager plan. William B. Munro, *Bibliography of Municipal Government* (Cambridge, Mass.: Harvard University Press, 1915), especially in Section 22, pp. 103–4, provides a good summary of important early writings on the council-manager plan.

Although they are long and tedious to read, the proceedings of the first six annual conferences of the City Manager Association published by the association in 1914, 1915, 1916, 1917–18, 1919, and 1920 serve as important resource materials for historians documenting the early development of this professional association. During the same period, the *American Political Science Review*, the *National Municipal Review*, and *American City* published articles on city management. All three journals were hot advocates of the manager plan, but the *American Political Science Review* took a somewhat more theoretical view than the other two journals. The best historic resource is, of course, the managers' own journal, first published in 1919 as the *City Manager Bulletin,* later called the *City Manager Magazine,* and in 1927 changed to its present title, *Public Management.* Especially during the late 1920s and early 1930s, *Public Management* became a first-class journal under the editorship of Clarence Ridley and Orin Nolting and included numerous articles by leading city managers of the period and university scholars such as William Mosher, Leonard White, A. R. Hatton, John Pfiffner, and Charles Merriam. Especially important during the 1920s and 1930s was the addition of the annual managers' association meeting proceedings to the journal. In 1934 the *Municipal Yearbook* began appearing annually. Published by the International City Management Association, it contains basic data on managers and their profession. Sections of the 1940, 1963, and 1964 yearbooks contain particularly extensive statistics on the city manager profession.

The Origin of the City Manager Plan in Staunton, Virginia (City of Staunton, 1954) is a surprisingly well-written account of why a small city adopted the first city manager plan. The complete list of articles by the early municipal reformers related to the council-manager plan is almost too long to cover in any bibliography but some of the representative reformers' essays on the subject are: H. G. James, "The City Manager Plan: The Latest in American Government," *American Political Science Review* (November 1914):89–94, 274–79; R. L. Fitzgerald, "The City Manager," *Journal of Western Society of Engineers* (May 1916):418–25; John Crosby, "Municipal Government Administered by a General Executive," *Annals of the American Academy of Political and Social Science* 38 (1911):877–78ff.; H. W. Dodds, "City Manager Government in American Municipalities," *Journal of Comparative Legislation* (November 1924):183–92; A. R. Hatton, "How the Manager Plan Works," Sixth Yearbook, *The Proceedings of the City Manager Association* (1920):113–18; L. D. Upson, "The City Manager Plan of Government for Dayton," *National Municipal Review* (1924):639ff.

Among the early reformers, the most devoted to promoting the manager idea throughout the country was Richard S. Childs. Don K. Price's short essay, "The Promotion of the City Manager Plan," *Public Opinion Quarterly* (Winter 1941):563–78 is an interpretative discussion of the way Childs influenced the early development of the manager idea. For a close analysis of the philosophy of Richard Childs with an extensive bibliography of his writings, refer to John Porter East, *Council-Manager Government: The Political Thought of Its Founder, Richard Childs* (Chapel Hill: University of North Carolina Press, 1965). Childs's own writings are much too numerous to cover completely in this bibliography, but some of his most representative works are *Civic Victories* (New York: Harper & Row, 1952); *The First 50 Years of the Council-Manager Plan of Municipal*

Government (New York: National Municipal League, 1965); "How the Commission-Manager Plan Is Getting Along," *National Municipal Review* (1915):371–82; "The New Profession of City Manager," *New Republic*, September 9, 1916, pp. 135–37; "The Future of the Commission-Manager Plan," *Modern City* (August 1918):19–21; "Professional Standards and Professional Ethics in the New Profession of City Manager," *National Municipal Review* (April 1916):195–210; "The City Manager Profession Up to Now," *City Manager Magazine* (November 1925):9–10; and "Looking Back at the City Managers Twenty Years Hence," *Public Management* (March 1937):80–82.

The books, articles, and journals cited above relate primarily to the pre–World War II phase of the development of the city management profession and the council-manager plan of government. They are valuable principally as historic references. Modern thought on the city management profession can be classified in two broad categories: first, writings that deal with internal professional problems; and second, writings that view the city manager from the outside or, in other words, provide different theoretical perspectives on the role, activities, and functions of the city manager. First let us examine the view from within the profession. Managers have discussed four major topics almost since the first meeting of the City Manager Association in 1914: (1) the role of the city manager in relationship to his council and community; (2) the education and training of city managers; (3) abandonments of the council-manager plan; and (4) relationships with various community individuals and civic groups. Early manager conventions and journals frequently had discussions on professional problems like tenure, licensing, and selection of managers, but these issues have become less prominent in recent years.

For the official position of the city manager association on the proper relationship of the manager to the council and the community in general, a study of the code of ethics as it was first adopted in 1924 and in its subsequent revised versions of 1938, 1952, and 1969 (see Appendix C) demonstrates clearly the shifting attitude toward the manager's role. Closer examination of individual manager and scholarly opinion shows a wider range of opinion on the subject. Several of the earliest writers closely equated the manager's role to that of a businessman; see Isaac F. Marcosson, "Business-Managing a City," *Colliers*, January 3, 1914, p. 5; J. S. Patton, "The Municipal Business Manager," *National Municipal Review* (January 1915):50–54. Several reformers, particularly Richard Childs, viewed the manager's role as that of making local government more democratic, honest, and "public regarding." See especially Childs's "Professional Standards and Professional Ethics in the New Profession of City Manager," *National Municipal Review* (April 1916):195–210, and his "Editorial," *Public Management* (February 1930):37. Several university scholars were impressed by the English model of the civil servant's role and argued that the manager should follow that example. The works already cited by Leonard White, Joseph Cohen, and A. R. Hatton seem to be influenced by this trend of thought. For an excellent statement of this philosophy from a prominent Englishman, refer to I. G. Gibbon, "Municipal Government in the United States: Some Impressions," *National Municipal Review* (February 1925):78–81.

Beginning in the 1920s, managers themselves stressed that their role concerned primarily the art and science of local management. For some of the best statements of this scientific management philosophy refer to: John N. Edy, "Managerial Functions of a Manager," *Public Management* (March 1926):51–62; O. E. Carr, "Progress, Prospects and Pitfalls of the New Profession of City Manager," *Canadian Engineer* (1918):513ff.; C. A. Bingham et al., "Management Problems of the City Manager," *Public Management* (March 1929):210–21; R. W. Rigsby, "The Technique of City Management," *Public Management* (March 1928):173–79; Clarence Ridley, "The Job of the City Manager," *Public Management* (September 1945):258–63. During the 1940s and 1950s management functions were still stressed, but emphasis shifted from the technical to the "coordinative" and cooperative: Frank L. Cloud, "Management Through Cooperation," *Public Management* (November 1942):2–6; John H. Ames, "The Art of Management," *Public Management* (January 1950):2–6; Julian H. Orr, "Personal and Financial Controls in Council-Manager Government," *The American City* (September 1953):100–101; John M. Pfiffner, "The Job of the City Manager," *Public Management* (June 1961):122–25; *The Technique of Municipal Administration* (Chicago: International City Managers' Association, 1958); George E. Bean, "Administrative Leadership," *Public Management* (February 1951):26–29; John M. Pfiffner, "Management Must Manage," *Public Management* (November 1953):242–45.

From the earliest managers' convention, some city managers always viewed their role in the widest possible context, as community leaders. The community leadership theme became a dominant theme among managers, after the 1948 presidential address by C. A. Harrell, city manager of Norfolk, Virginia at the Thirty-fourth Manager Convention, Mackinac Island, Michigan. Important statements of the leadership role in public policy are: Harry Freeman, "Selling Government to the People," *City Manager Magazine* (May 1920):1928–29; Louis Brownlow, "The Human Element in City Administration," *Public Management* (March 1929):283–84; C. A. Harrell, "The City Manager as a Community Leader," *Public Management* (October 1948):290–94; "Leadership Functions of the City Manager," discussion by various city managers, *Public Management* (June 1949):162–67; C. A. Harrell and D. G. Wieford, "The City Manager and the Policy Process," *Public Administration Review* (Spring 1959):101–7; John M. Biery et al., "Leadership Functions of the Manager," *Public Management* (March 1955):50–54; Woodbury Brackett, "The

Changing Role of the City Manager," *Public Management* (January 1962): 2–3; Nathan D. Grundstein, "What is Meant by Leadership?" *Public Management* (November 1962):242–46. For an extreme viewpoint by a political scientist that the city manager is a politician, read Karl Bosworth, "The Manager is a Politician," *Public Administration Review* (Summer 1959):216–20.

Education and training of city managers has been another subject of considerable professional interest. Since the 1920s important members of the academic community have frequently discussed the subject; see Chester C. Maxey, "The Training of City Managers," *National Municipal Review* (March 1920):142–45; Dr. William E. Mosher, "Training for the Public Service," *Public Management* (April 1928):325–28; Clarence E. Ridley, "Report of the Committee on Curriculum," *Public Management* (March 1929):131–36; Thomas H. Reed, "Training for the Public Service," *American Political Science Review, Supplement* (1930):173–79; Leonard White et al., "Final Report on the Committee on Training for the City Manager Profession," *Public Management* (May 1931):157–59: John C. Bollens, "Municipal Management Training," *Public Management* (July 1950):146–49; Arthur W. Bromage, "Preparing Future City Managers," *Public Management* (April 1950):74–76; Edwin O. Stene, "University Training for City Management," *Public Management* (January 1952):6–9. Several current and well-documented studies of the subject are: L. P. Cookingham et al., *City Management—A Growing Profession* (Chicago: International City Managers' Association, 1957); Robert L. Brunton and William E. Besuden, *Internship Training for City Managers* (Chicago: International City Managers' Association, 1960); *Post Entry Training in Local Public Service* (Chicago: International City Managers' Association, 1963); Stephen B. Sweeney et al., *Education for Administrative Careers in Government Service* (Philadelphia: University of Pennsylvania Press, 1958); *Training for the Public Service: Council-Management Government* (Urbana: Institute of Government and Public Affairs, University of Illinois, 1955). Edwin O. Stene, *The City Manager: Professional Training and Tenure* (Lawrence, Kans.: University of Kansas Press, 1966); Orin F. Nolting, "Training America's City Managers," *Municipal and Public Service Journal* (October 21, 1966):34ff.; Stephen B. Sweeney, "The Professional Development of Urban Managers," mimeographed paper (Chicago: International City Managers' Association, 1965). For an early manager's comments against professional training for managers, refer to the remarks by Charles Ashburner as quoted by Joseph Cohen, "The City Manager as a Profession," *National Municipal Review Supplement* (July 1924):401. For a more recent, lively critique of management training programs, read William V. Donaldson, "Continuing Education for City Managers," *Public Administration Review* (November/December 1973): 504–7.

Abandonments of council-manager government have been a third major area of professional concern. Recent studies on this include: Edwin O. Stene and George K. Floro, *Abandonments of the Manager Plan* (Lawrence, Kans.: University of Kansas Press, 1953); Arthur Bromage, *Manager Plan Abandonments* (New York: National Municipal League, 1964); Eugene W. Kimmel, *The Abandonment of Council-Manager Government by South Dakota Municipalities* (Vermillion: University of South Dakota, 1966); Roger D. Hoffmaster, *The Abandonment of the Council-Manager Plan Among Third-Class Cities in the State of Missouri* (Parkville, Mo.: Park College, 1958); Kent Quinn, *Brookfield, Missouri Abandons the Council-Manager Plan* (Parkville, Mo.: Park College, 1960). The most analytic and carefully documented report was produced by the ICMA, *Council-Manager Plan Abandonments* (Chicago: International City Managers' Association, 1964).

Particularly since 1950, the subject that has appeared to have the greatest professional interest is the relationship between managers and various community groups and individuals. The list of articles is too long to cover fully, but the most significant ones include: L. C. Reithmayer, "Relations of the City Manager with Pressure Groups," *Public Management* (January 1954):2–5; Allen Grimes, "The Job of the City Manager and the City Attorney," *Public Management* (February 1959):38–42; Frank P. Sherwood, "Roles of the City Manager and the Police," *Public Management* (May 1959):110–13; Jeptha Carrel, "The City Manager and His Council: Sources of Conflict," *Public Administration Review* (December 1962):203–8; Clarence O. Schlaver, "The Manager and the Mayor," *Public Management* (February 1966):59–69; Michigan Municipal League, *The Michigan City Manager in Council Proceedings* (Ann Arbor: Michigan Municipal League, 1960); W. I. Goodman, "The Planner's Relationship with the City Manager," *Journal of the American Institute of Planners* (Summer 1953):147–50; L. P. Cookingham, "The Relationship of the City Manager and Finance Officer," *Texas Town and City* (August 1961):8–10; John E. Dever et al., "Relations of the Manager with the Public," *Public Management* (April 1955):77–83; A. A. Meredith, "Press Relations in City Management," *Public Management* (December 1951):272–73; "Relations with Employee Organizations," *Public Management* (January 1956):2–7; George E. Bean et al., "Organized Labor and the Council-Manager Plan," *Public Management* (June 1951):122–32; James Weinstein, "Organized Business and the City Commission and Manager Movements," *Journal of Southern History* (May 1962):166–82; Thomas W. Kressbach, *The Michigan City Manager in Budgetary Proceedings* (Ann Arbor: Michigan Municipal League, 1962); Richard A. Salvati, *The Role of the City Manager in Communicating to the Public* (Ann Arbor: Michigan Municipal League, 1966); Deil Wright and Robert Boynton, "The Media, the Masses, & Urban Management," *Journalism Quarterly* (Spring 1970):12–19; Deil

Wright and Paul Boynton, "Mayor-Manager Relationships in Large
Council-Manager Cities: A Reinterpretation," *Public Administration
Review* (January/February 1971):28–35; and Deil Wright, "Intergovernmental Relations in Large Council-Manager Cities," paper presented at the 1970 Southwestern Political Science Association, Dallas, Texas,
March 26, 1970. Three outstanding articles have examined the relationship
of the city manager to the courts: John M. Pfiffner, "The City Manager and
the Courts," *Public Management* (July 1930):387–94 and (August
1930):425–29; and Charles M. Kneier, "The City Manager and the Courts,
1930–50," *Public Management* (July 1951):148–52.

The second major body of literature on the city manager examines him
from a variety of different viewpoints. It includes: (1) studies of the
manager as part of the council-manager plan; (2) personal diaries; (3) case
studies; (4) community power studies; (5) role analyses; (6) professional
interpretations.

Since 1945 numerous state and local studies of the council-manager plan
have included scattered references to city managers. They have frequently
been published by local state bureaus of municipal research and so are
sometimes heavily biased in favor of the manager plan. While this
reformist literature is of uneven quality, some of it is worth examining,
since it often gives a unique perspective on the manager working as part of
the council-manager plan. One of the best of these studies is John C.
Bollens, *Appointed Executive Local Government* (Los Angeles: Haynes
Foundation, 1952). This book includes a particularly good analysis of the
differences between city managers and chief administrative officers in
California (especially refer to Chaps. 4 and 5, pp. 88–137). Other similar
writings are: B. H. Stringham and D. W. James, *The Utah Experience with
the Council-Manager Idea* (Salt Lake City: University of Utah, 1947);
William O. Farber, *City Manager Government in South Dakota* (Vermillion: University of South Dakota, 1948); W. F. Larson, *The Council-
Manager Plan in Florida: The Theory and Practice* (Gainesville: University
of Florida Press, 1953); Dorothy I. Cline, *Albuquerque and the City
Manager Plan* (Albuquerque: University of New Mexico Press, 1951); C. L.
Ringgenberg, *Council-Manager Government in Iowa* (Iowa City: Univer-
sity of Iowa, 1953); Paul Kelso, *A Decade of Council Manager Government
in Phoenix, Arizona* (Phoenix: City Council of Phoenix, 1960); Robert J.
Frye and John A. Dyer, *The City Manager System in Alabama* (University,
Ala.: University of Alabama, 1961); James Wilson and Robert W. Crowe,
Managers in Maine (Brunswick, Me.: Bowdoin College, 1961); Ruth Y.
Wetmore, *Council and Commission Manager Government in Kansas*
(Lawrence, Kans.: University of Kansas, 1961); *Texas Council-Manager
Charters* (Austin: University of Texas, 1961); *The Council Manager Form of
Government in Pennsylvania* (Pittsburgh: University of Pittsburgh, 1963);
Kay G. Collett and Henry M. Alexander, *The City Manager Plan in*

Arkansas (Fayetteville: University of Arkansas, 1966); Iola Hessler, *29 Ways to Govern a City* (Cincinnati: Hamilton County Research Foundation, 1966).

An interesting view of the city manager's work is found by reading personal diaries of individual managers. Unfortunately few of these have been published. One humorous account of what it was like to assume a city manager's post in San Jose, California in 1916 is by Thomas H. Reed, "Trends in City Management," *Public Management* (December 1955):266–71. Other interesting diaries include: W. P. Hunter, "A Day in a City Manager's Office," *Public Management* (August 1934):240–42; A. W. Wedslye, "A Day in the City Manager's Life," *Public Management* (July 1937):199–202. For several current diaries refer to the section on case histories, pp. 26–32, in *Guideposts on Assuming a City Manager's Position* (Chicago: International City Managers' Association, 1958). For perhaps the best personal statement, refer to Louis Brownlow, *A Passion for Anonymity* (Chicago: University of Chicago Press, 1958), parts I and II.

Case histories written in the third person on a city manager's work are more numerous. Several have been written for the purpose of training managers: refer especially to Edwin O. Stene, *Case Problems in City Management* (Chicago: International City Managers' Association, 1964). For more general studies that emphasize the city manager's role in policy issues, see: Frank C. Abbot, "The Cambridge City Manager," in Harold Stein, ed., *Public Administration and Policy Development: A Case Book* (New York: Harcourt Brace, 1952); Frank P. Sherwood, *A City Manager Tries to Fire His Police Chief* (Syracuse: Inter-University Case Program, 1963); Beverly L. Browning, *North Kingstown Selects Two Town Managers, A Case Study* (Kingstown: University of Rhode Island, 1962); John Bartlow Martin, "The Town That Reformed," *Saturday Evening Post*, October 1, 1955, p. 16; Bruce Kovner, "The Resignation of Elgin Crull," in Edward Banfield, ed., *Urban Government: A Reader in Administration and Politics* (New York: Free Press, 1969), pp. 316–22; Warner E. Mills and Harry R. Davis, *Small City Government* (New York: Random House, 1962); and James Wilson, "Manager Under Fire," in Richard T. Frost, ed., *Cases in State and Local Government* (Englewood Cliffs, N.J.: Prentice-Hall, 1961).

Community power studies frequently portray the city manager as a central actor. For several interesting references from this perspective, refer to: Albert and Ruth Schaffer, *Woodruff: A Study of Community Decision-Making* (Chapel Hill: University of North Carolina Press, 1970); Aaron Wildavsky, *Leadership in a Small Town* (Totowa, N.J.: Bedminster Press, 1964); Oliver Williams and Charles Adrian, *Four Cities: A Study in Comparative Policy Making* (Philadelphia: University of Pennsylvania Press, 1963); David Greenstone, *A Report on Politics in San Diego* (Cambridge: Joint Center for Urban Studies, 1962); M. Kent Jennings,

Community Influentials (New York: Free Press, 1964). Several short articles dealing with the subject are J. A. Vieg, "The Manager Plan and the Metropolitan Community," *American Political Science Review* (February 1939):69–80; W. D. Lockard, "City Manager Administrative Theory and Political Power," *Political Science Quarterly* (June 1962):224–36; Charles Adrian, "Leadership and Decision Making in Manager Cities: A Study of Three Communities," *Public Administration Review* (Summer 1958): 212–16; William A. Sommers, "Council-Manager Government: A Review," *Western Political Science Quarterly* (March 1958):137–48. Four empirical analyses of the characteristics of council-manager cities and their effects on policy outcomes are: Edgar L. Sherbenou, "Class, Participation, and the Council-Manager Plan," *Public Administration Review* (Summer 1961):131–35; Leo F. Schnore and Robert R. Alford, "Forms of Government and the Socioeconomic Characteristics of Suburbs," *Administrative Science Quarterly* (June 1963):1–17; John H. Kessel, "Government Structure and Political Environment," *The American Political Science Review* (September 1962):615–20; Robert L. Lineberry and Edmund P. Fowler, "Reformism and Public Policies in American Cities," *The American Political Science Review* (September 1967):701–16.

Closely related to the community power studies are role analyses of the city manager. These writings focus in greater detail on the manager's characteristics, attitudes, and activities in relationship to other community leaders: B. James Kweder, *The Roles of the City Manager, Mayor and Councilmen in Policy Making: A Study of 21 North Carolina Cities* (Chapel Hill: University of North Carolina Press, 1965); Gladys Kammerer et al., *The Urban Political Community: Profiles in Town Politics* (Boston: Houghton Mifflin Co., 1963); Gladys Kammerer et al., *City Managers in Politics: An Analysis of Manager Tenure and Termination,* University of Florida Monographs (Gainesville: Winter 1962); John C. Buechner, *Differences in Role Perceptions in Council-Manager Cities* (Boulder: University of Colorado, 1965); Jeptha Carrell, *The Role of the City Manager* (Lawrence, Kans.: University of Kansas, 1962). Numerous short articles are found on this subject, particularly in recent years; see Lloyd M. Wells, "Social Values and Political Orientation of City Managers," *Southwestern Social Science Quarterly* (December 1967):443–50; David Booth, "Are Elected Mayors a Threat to Managers?" *Administrative Science Quarterly* (March 1968):572–90; George Floro, "Types of City Managers," *Public Management* (October 1952):218ff.; Jeptha J. Carrell, "The Role of the City Manager: A Survey Report," *Public Management* (April 1962):74–78; M. Kent Jennings, "Public Administrators and Community Decision-Making," *Administrative Science Quarterly* (Winter 1964):18–43; Gladys M. Kammerer, "Role Diversity of City Managers," *Administrative Science Quarterly* (Winter 1963):421–42; Ronald O. Loveridge, "City Managers in Legislative Politics," *Polity* (Winter 1968):

213–36; Deil S. Wright, "The City Manager as a Development Administrator," in Robert T. Doland, ed., *Comparative Urban Research: The Administration and Politics of Cities* (Beverly Hills, Calif.: Sage Publications, 1969), pp. 203–48.

Finally, the professional view of city managers was a dominant theme of writers in the 1920s and early 1930s, particularly the works already cited by Leonard White, Joseph Cohen, Clarence Ridley, and Orin Nolting. Official pamphlets and writings of the ICMA frequently stressed the professional theme but at rather an unsophisticated level. In the late 1960s, however, five books appeared that restated in different ways the professional theme of the earlier writers: an examination of training and tenure of city managers, Edwin O. Stene, *The City Manager: Professional Training and Tenure* (Lawrence, Kans.: University of Kansas, 1966); a study of the development of the International City Management Association, Orin F. Nolting, *Progress and Impact of the Council-Manager Plan* (Chicago: Public Administration Service, 1969); a book on city managers in Oklahoma by David R. Morgan and Harvey W. Seward II, *The Oklahoma City Manager Profession: A 1968 Profile* (Norman: University of Oklahoma, 1968); a short but thoughtful essay by John Bollens and John C. Ries, *The City Manager Profession: Myths and Realities* (Chicago: Public Administration Service, 1969); and particularly Chaps. 4 and 5 of James M. Banovetz, ed., *Managing the Modern City* (Washington: International City Management Association, 1971). An excellent study is Richard B. Vogel, "The Origin, Growth and Development of the International City Managers' Association" (Ph.D. diss., University of Iowa, 1967), available at the ICMA headquarters in Washington. David S. Arnold did the most recent quantitative profile on city managers; it appeared in "A Profile of City Managers," *Public Management* (March 1964):56–60 and in the same journal (September 1964):264ff. Alva Stewart surveyed seven female city managers in "Women in City Management," *Municipal South* (January 1963):20–22. Two of the most recent journal-length discussions of the city management profession are in *Public Management* (May 1970) and the *Public Administration Review* (January/February 1971). For an interesting account of the ICMA's relationship with the academic community and of current urban research requirements, read *Long-Range Program for Urban Management Research* (Chicago: International City Managers' Association, 1964). Norton Long, "Politicians for Hire," *Public Administration Review* (June 1965):115–20, provides an excellent political interpretation of professional managers.

For three classic debates over the applicability of professional management to large American cities, refer to: A. R. Hatton and Bradley Hull, "A Debate—Is City Manager Government Applicable to Our Largest Cities?" *Eighth Yearbook of the City Manager Association* (1922), pp. 225–48; and more recently the debate between Wallace S. Sayre, "The General

Manager Idea for Large Cities," *Public Administration Review* (Autumn 1954):253–58, and John E. Bebout, "Management for Large Cities," *Public Administration Review* (Summer 1955):188–95; and *The Rotarian Magazine* (September 1962).

Major textbooks on municipal government normally devote one or two chapters to council-manager government. A glance at several of the prominent texts published since 1920 offers a unique overview of how prominent university scholars have examined the city manager. In William B. Munro, *Municipal Government and Administration* (New York: Macmillan Co., 1923), the historic development and legal structure of the council-manager plan received the greatest attention. In both Lent D. Upson, *Practices of Municipal Administration* (New York: Century Co., 1926) and Thomas H. Reed, *Municipal Management* (New York: McGraw-Hill, 1941) good city government was closely identified with the qualities of good management technique, which both books attempted to describe in detail. The manager was, of course, represented as the expert in this activity and therefore occupied a venerated position. Both Arthur Bromage, *Introduction to Municipal Government and Administration* (New York: Appleton-Century-Crofts, 1950) and Austin F. MacDonald, *American City Government and Administration* (New York: Thomas Y. Crowell Co., 1956) devote two chapters to council-manager government and give a sophisticated reformist view of the manager as an individual responsible for carrying out the policy dictates of council. Edward C. Banfield and James Q. Wilson, *City Politics* (Cambridge, Mass.: Harvard University Press, 1963) perceive the city manager in a radically different way. Drawing heavily on case studies and community power analyses, the authors view the manager no longer as the neutral instrument of the council, but rather as a political actor whose own authority depends directly on the distribution of community power. The policy activities of the manager are stressed over his managerial role in the community.

For several studies of the concept applied in countries outside the United States, refer to: Arthur W. Bromage, "The Council-Manager Plan in Ireland," *Public Management* (February 1961):26–32; Aarne Eskola, "The Council-Manager Plan in Finland," *Public Management* (February 1960):33–35; B. P. Gupta, "Council-Manager Plan of American Cities: Its Application to India," *Quarterly Journal of the Local Self-Government Institute* (April–June 1962):479–86; Walther Hensel, "The Council-Manager Plan in Germany," *Public Management* (January 1961):2–5; John M. McIver, "A Survey of the City Manager Plan in Canada," *Canadian Public Administration* (September 1960):216–32; Robert L. Morlan, "City Manager Contrasts: The Netherland Experience," *Public Administration Review* (Spring 1962):65–70; and Orin F. Nolting, "The Council-Manager Plan in Europe," *Public Management* (May 1958):110–14.

For a recent comprehensive bibliography on council-manager government, refer to: *Council-Manager Government, 1940–64: An Annotated Bibliography* (Chicago: International City Managers' Association, 1965). It was compiled by David Booth of the University of Kentucky for the ICMA. For the two most recent discussions of the city manager, see the entire issues of *Public Management* (May 1970) and *Public Administration Review* (January/February 1971). Also for an excellent recent empirical study of the city manager as a political actor in the policy-making process of communities, see Ronald O. Loveridge *City Managers in Legislative Politics* (Indianapolis: Bobbs-Merrill Co., 1971).

Index

A. E. Chew Company, 136
Abbot, Frank C., 60, 157
academic community: council-manager plan supported by, 21–22; ICMA's relationship to, 63–64, 68, 136, 159; scientific management supported by, 45–46
administration, as role of city manager, 3, 40, 42–43, 56–57, 88, 107, 152–53. *See also* merit system of personnel administration; public administration
Administrative Behavior (Simon), 55
administrative generalist, city manager as, 81–82
administrative officer. *See* Chief Administrative Officer
Administrative State, The (Waldo), 55
Adrian, Charles R., 2, 25, 107, 157
Alexander, Henry M., 156
Alford, Robert R., 105, 158
Alger, Horatio, 7, 18
Amarillo, Tex., 30
American City Bureau (U.S. Chamber of Commerce), 31–32, 33
American Cyanamid Company, 136
American Foreign Service, 86ff.; city managers, role comparison with, 85ff.; education requirements, 88–89; elitism in, 91–92, 96–97; formation of, 86–87, 145; ideology, 90, 97; structure, organizational, 89–90, 91; structure, social, 87–88, 91–92
American Government, The (Haskin), 48
American Legislators Association, 46
American Management Association, 64
American Municipal Association, 46
American Public Welfare Association, 46
American Public Works Association, 46
American Smelting and Refining, 7
American Society of Municipal Engineers, 7
American Society of Planning Officials, 46
Americans for Democratic Action (ADA), 63
Ames, John H., 57
Anderson, William, 22
Annals of the American Academy of Political and Social Science, 36
Appleby, Paul H., 55
Arlington, Va., 74
Arnold, David S., 159
"Art of Management, The" (Ames), 57

Ashburner, Charles E., 14, 30, 40, 43, 107, 114, 154
at-large elections, as reform technique, 28

Bailey, Stephen K., 148
Baltimore, Md., 93
Banfield, Edward C., 106, 107, 157, 160
Banovetz, James M., 159
Bauer, David, 143
Bean, George E., 2, 153, 155
Beard, Charles A., 9, 16, 18, 20, 36, 45
Bebout, John E., 116, 160
Beck, E. A., 34
Berkeley, Calif., 42
Biery, John M., 153
Bingham, C. A., 37, 153
Bloomington, Ind., 102
Bluefield, Va., 46
Bollens, John C., 103, 154, 156, 159
Bon Ami Company, 15, 19, 136
Booth, David, 158, 161
Boston, Mass., 115; Chief Administrative Officer in, 25, 66; school superintendent, employment in, 93
Bosworth, Karl, 61, 104, 154
Boynton, Paul, 156
Boynton, Robert, 155
Brackett, Woodbury, 153
Bradford, Ernest S., 18
Braxton, Hugh C., 14
Bromage, Arthur W., 154, 155, 160
Browning, Beverly, 157
Brownlow, Louis, 28, 33, 37–38, 43, 45–46, 47–49, 51, 53, 57, 66, 115, 124, 153, 157
Bruere, H. J., 20
Bryce, James, 15
Buechner, John C., 158
business administrator. *See* Chief Administrative Officer
business ideals, 7–8; Childs's adherence to, 15, 17, 136; council-manager plan influenced by, 8, 12, 20–21, 26; decline of confidence in, 55; democracy and, 17; education, role in, 95–96; government, role in, 14, 20–21; in school superintendent profession, 95–96

California Municipalities, 14
Callahan, Raymond E., 95

162